Gennifer Flowers

Gennifer Flowers

Passion and Betrayal

Gennifer Flowers

with

Jacquelyn Dapper

Emery Dalton Books
Del Mar, California

Library of Congress Catalog Card Number:

94-69406

ISBN 0-9640479-3-4

Emery Dalton Books
1110 Camino Del Mar, Suite C
Del Mar, CA 92014

Printed in the United States of America

10 9 8 7 6 5 4 3 2 1

This book is dedicated to the millions of women everywhere who gave their hearts, shared their souls, and suffered the heartbreak of loving a married man. We know each other's pain so well.

And it is dedicated also to the genuine seekers of truth in this great land, for without their courage and steadfast determination, that which lies beyond the horizon can only be tyranny.

Acknowledgments

Thanks so much to these wonderful people, without whose love and support this book would not have been possible:

My parents, Mary and Jim Hirst, for their unconditional love and encouragement.

Finis, for his support and creative contributions.

Finis' mother, Emma Shelnutt, and his two daughters, Maria and Jennifer, for their love and support.

Marjorie Moore, for her friendship, unwavering loyalty, and her marvelous sense of humor that kept me going.

The few members of my large family who stood by me and loved me through all the turmoil: Uncle Curtis R. Horne, Sr., who passed away on May 17, 1994, Aunt Aliene Horne, Uncle Jim Lance, Aunt Dot and Uncle Harlen Moore, Cousins Suzanne and Elisa Hawkins, Cousin Billy Frank Lance, and Cousin Jerry Flowers.

Jay Wallace and all my friends in Fort Worth, Texas, for their understanding and caring hospitality.

Gregg Gunter, Dan Cassurella, Tracy Sheldon, Karen Clinton, and Betty Biggerstaff, for their loyal friendship and support.

My Hollywood pals: Jane Keane and Ruta Lee, for their advice and friendship.

Morton Downey Jr., Howard Stern, and especially Barry Farber, who gave me a friendly forum to discuss my story.

All the folks in Brinkley, Arkansas, and especially a few '68 classmates who stood by "Little Geannie Flowers."

Blake Hendrix, for his guidance, professionalism, and continuing friendship.

My collaborators, Vicki Gibbs and Jackie Dapper, for their talent, expertise, and hard work.

David Levine, for his insight and creative input.

My publishers, Michael Dalton Johnson and Mark Fleming, who believed in me and this book and never wavered in their support.

And a very special thanks to my agent, Ed Menken, who defended this "Shiksa's" right to tell her story. I will be forever grateful for his outstanding creative contribution to this project, his professionalism, and unquestionable friendship during the hard times.

Contents

Prologue

On a warm summer evening in 1977, Arkansas Attorney General Bill Clinton stepped off a plane at Little Rock Airport. Little did I know that the next sixty seconds would start a chain of events that would forever alter the course of my life.

I was working as a television news reporter and had been sent to interview Mr. Clinton about a meeting he and Arkansas Senator Dale Bumpers had just attended in Washington. Although the sun had set, the air was still warm—but I was shivering from nervousness. I wasn't intimidated by Mr. Clinton—he had the reputation of being open and friendly, a man who would greet you with a handshake and a smile. I was nervous because I was new. In fact, I had been with the station for only a few weeks, and this was my first major assignment.

Clinton walked briskly toward the little group of reporters. He seemed in a buoyant mood. We all raised our hands at once, and through the chorus of questions, I asked in a loud voice, "Mr. Clinton, can I get a statement from you?" He turned to the sound of my voice and locked his eyes on me. He walked straight over to me with a big grin growing on his face, gave me a casual once-over, and asked, with his now-familiar Arkansas drawl, "*Where* did they get *you?*"

For an instant I was speechless. Here I was, trying to do my job, and the attorney general was coming on to me! I looked at him innocently, pretending not to understand what he was implying, and quickly replied, "I just started recently." Then, before he had a chance to say anything else, I plunged right into my questions. Although he gave serious answers, that lazy, sexy smile never left his face. His light blue eyes stayed focused on mine, as though we were the only ones on the tarmac. He was clearly sending me a strong message and it had nothing to do with my questions.

I breathed a sigh of relief when he left. I felt drained. Although I was a little put off by his come-on, I had to admit he was attractive: tall—well over six feet—dark, wavy hair; bedroom eyes; and the sexiest mouth I had ever seen. Was this just a game he played with women, or did he actually have an interest in me?

What was I thinking! Bill Clinton was a public figure and a powerful man in Arkansas. He was also very married. I shook my head and came to my senses.

For several weeks after our first meeting, whenever I covered a story that involved him, he would spot me, even in the most crowded rooms, and give me that sexy stare. Everyone noticed, but he didn't seem to care. When the press was waiting for a statement, he would single me out of the crowd and deliberately speak to me first.

I admit, I was flattered. But it was also becoming embarrassing. My colleagues were starting to resent the special treatment I was getting. So even though I actually began to enjoy his little games, I really did try to discourage him. When he would stare at me, I would glare back at him, sending him a silent message to stop. But this only seemed to encourage him. His obvious focus on me was starting to cause whispers and rumors throughout the capitol and at the TV station. But Bill seemed oblivious to the talk.

For the next few weeks he played a game of psychological foreplay with me, and there was no doubt the chemistry between us was building. He had captured my interest, but the obvious complications were never far from my mind. This was trouble, and I knew it.

Yet, I found Bill Clinton incredibly sexy. I can still remember the way he had of staring at me. He did more than just mentally undress me—he was visually seducing me, and he made sure I knew it. He was turning me upside down and inside out just by looking at me, and when he looked away, I almost felt as though we had just made love. I was breathless and more than a little uneasy.

He finally made his move in the lobby of the Justice Building. Once again, I was waiting for a statement. My cameraman was just outside the building. Bill came walking through the lobby, and when he caught sight of me he came right over. Without hesitation he whispered, "I don't know about you, but I can't stand this anymore. I just have to see you. Would you give me your phone number?"

I panicked. I knew my cameraman would walk through the door any moment, and he or anyone else could overhear us. One part of me was glad he had asked because I was feeling a tremendous attraction to him. But another part was struggling with all those complications. I rationalized, "I can give this guy my number and then I don't have to take his calls, or I can brush him off later." So I quickly tore a page from my notebook, scribbled down my number, and handed it to him.

When he called the next day and asked if he could come see me, I knew I should say no. But he was so charming and sexy. So I agreed to let him come to my apartment since we couldn't meet in public.

Waiting for him to arrive that night, I was nervous as a cat. First I sat. Then I stood. Then I paced back and forth in my tiny living room. When the doorbell finally rang, I jumped. As I opened the door, I saw him standing there with that friendly smile and those probing eyes staring right into mine. But in no time at all he put me at ease. He was relaxed and casual, and to my great relief, didn't even glance toward the bedroom.

We sat down opposite each other at a table in my tiny living room. He was so wonderful that I felt totally at ease. We talked for hours, just like old friends. He seemed truly interested in my opinions, which impressed me.

We talked and drank a little wine. He had a great sense of humor, and I relaxed further. I realized he wasn't going to make any sudden moves on me. That made him even more desirable. Now and then he'd reach across the table and gently hold my hand, rubbing it a little and sending little sparks of electricity through me. When he wanted to make a particular point about something, he would drop my hand and touch my leg. It wasn't like a come-on; it was more a demonstration of his passion for whatever subject we were discussing. It all felt very natural.

I liked Bill. He was an intelligent, good-looking, passionate man who seemed interested in me as a person. His apparent desire to get to know me, rather that what was underneath my clothes, really pleased me.

I could have talked all night, but it was getting late and I had to get up early to do the weather. It was time for him to go.

He didn't protest as I walked him to the door. He just turned and gave me a kiss—not passionate, just sweet and gentle. My heart fluttered and I thought. "This is nice. I like this." The complications of course were still there, but they just didn't seem to matter as much now. We'd had a extraordinary evening, and I felt good about him—and about myself. He managed to put my fears to rest.

Prologue

Looking back now, I believe he consciously manipulated me that first evening we spent together. He is an expert with women. He played me like a violin that night.

It worked, too. By the time he phoned me the next day, I was hooked. I couldn't wait to see him again. We made plans to meet at my apartment again. Like the first time, my heart was pounding as I waited for the doorbell to ring. This time, however, it was with desire. All that luscious verbal and visual foreplay, and yet we'd hardly touched. Now, I wanted to feel his touch so much I could almost feel his hands on my skin . . . .

One

Bill Clinton is a tremendously sexual man. You can see it in his eyes . . . in his smile . . . in the way he holds his head as he listens intently to what you have to say. I saw that the first time I met him back in 1977. What I didn't see or have any inkling of was the stupendous impact this man was going to have on my life.

I had no way of knowing then that he would one day be president of the United States. When we met, he was the thirty-one-year-old attorney general of Arkansas, an important, but not particularly impressive position. I was a twenty-seven-year-old singer and a news reporter for a Little Rock television station. In fact, at that time I probably had more of a local celebrity status than he did, as I had been singing in clubs around town for several years.

One thing I did know about him . . . he was married. Because of that, I tried to discourage the obvious advances he made to me every time I was sent to cover a meeting or event that he was hosting or attending. But his attraction was too strong, and eventually we wound up in my bed, giving in to feelings that had been building in both of us.

That was the beginning of a passionate, loving relationship that lasted twelve years and followed me through moves to different cities and even a year of traveling as a back-up singer with the Roy Clark Show. It survived through Bill's long term as governor of Arkansas and through the birth of his daughter, Chelsea. It might still be going on if I hadn't found a man I really wanted to share the rest of my life with.

Even after our physical relationship ended, he asked me if we could stay in touch over the phone, and we did, calling each other to share details of our separate lives. After all, we had many beautiful, erotic memories together. And they might have remained just that—our private memories—if fate hadn't intervened in the form of a muddy presidential election. Once Bill announced his candidacy, both our lives changed forever. The national media descended on Little Rock, digging everywhere they could to uncover some dirt on this little-known southern politician from the backwoods state of Arkansas. And, boy, did they find dirt.

Soon, I was being hounded by print, television, and radio reporters to tell them my story . . . corroborate the evidence they thought they had on Bill Clinton and his affairs. But I wanted no part of it. I refused to take their calls or answer their questions. I just wanted to be left alone to get on with my life . . . until a string of events woke me up to the fact that I needed to protect myself, in more ways than one. First, my personal safety and security were threatened when someone broke into and ransacked my apartment. I was certain it was somehow connected to my relationship with Bill. Next, it became obvious that, because of all the publicity I was receiving, I would be unable to continue in the state job I had been depending on for a second income since the entertainment business had slowed down in the early '90s. And last, it was clear I wasn't even going to be able to remain in Arkansas, the state that I had called home since I was a little girl.

All of that combined made me decide to cooperate with the tabloid *Star* in a two-part story about Bill Clinton and me. They were already planning on printing a story with or without my corroboration, and they were willing to pay me if I agreed to help. I hoped that my working with them on the story would ensure that the information was accurate. And they did a pretty good job of reporting the facts. Since then, much has been written and said about me and my relationship with Bill . . . most of it false. This is partly due to the fact that Bill's spin doctors undertook a major character assassination campaign when they realized I might stand in the way of his getting elected. That's why I wanted to write this book, to tell the story as is really happened.

In spite of all the negative things that have happened to me as a result of my relationship with Bill, I still have warm feelings toward him. In fact, this book is really a love story, with large doses of passion and ultimately of betrayal. But most important, it's the truth.

# # #

Eura Gean Flowers. That's the name my daddy chose for me when I was born. He created the name in honor of two people he really cared about—my godmother and an army buddy. Mother agreed to it with the understanding that I would never be called by that name. So, while I was growing up, I was always known as Geannie Flowers.

When I started singing professionally as an adult, Geannie sounded a little unsophisticated to me and not in keeping with the image I wanted to project. The thought of being introduced as "Little Geannie Flowers," made me shudder. I decided it was time to create a stage name. Mother and I were tossing around different possibilities one day, and I told her how I'd always liked the name "Jennifer." She said, "Why not use Jennifer, but spell it with a 'G'?" I liked the idea—I had been Geannie with a "G," so why not Gennifer with a "G"? So I had my name changed legally to Gennifer Flowers.

It's surprising how a little thing like that can have repercussions later in your life. When reporters and Bill Clinton's spin doctors started trying to discredit me, they searched everywhere they could to find cracks in my story. When they contacted the University of Arkansas about my records, they were told no one by the name of Gennifer Flowers had ever been enrolled there. They took that to mean I was lying about that and therefore must be lying about other things as well. They didn't bother to search far enough to find that I was registered there under my birth name, Eura Gean.

Mother and Daddy were both Okies—Mother from Dougherty, Oklahoma, and Daddy from Atoka. My dad, Gene Flowers, was one of seven children; his mother died in childbirth when he was only three or four years old. He went to live with his grandparents, but from there he was shuffled around a lot. As soon as he saw a way to get out into the world on his own, he did.

Airplanes always fascinated Daddy. When he was just a kid, he'd hang around the airport, watching the airplanes take off and land. Finally, when he was fourteen, someone taught him how to fly, and he turned that skill into a career. He was an army pilot during World War II, and after the war he continued working as a pilot wherever he lived. Planes were a big part of our life, and we used them the way most people use cars.

Daddy was Clark Gable handsome, tall and well built. He wasn't well educated as far as I know—he never really would say—and I'm not even sure he graduated from high school. He was a self-made man, and by the time he was killed, he was a millionaire.

Mother came from a large family, too. She was one of *thirteen* children. Like my father, she grew up in circumstances that were typical of the times. Both my parents were from big families that never had a lot of money, and all the kids participated in running the household.

Daddy's good looks and outgoing, rakish personality made him real appealing to women. He had that certain "look" in his eye, and he turned into quite a womanizer. This habit eventually drove my mother to divorce him, but he couldn't resist women, and they couldn't resist him. I know my mother certainly couldn't. After I met Bill Clinton, I thought many times about the similarities between him and my daddy. Bill had that same twinkle in his eye, which got the same response from women.

Mother was going to business college in Dallas when she and Daddy met. She also had a part-time job in a drugstore. He would come into the drugstore and immediately dominate the room with his good looks and self confidence, drawing women to him. Mother was petite and pretty and she didn't pay him the same attention the other girls did, which really intrigued him. He kept coming in, trying his best to charm her, and she finally gave in and accepted a date with him. Daddy didn't have a car, only a motorcycle and an airplane. So when they went out, more often than not it was in his airplane.

Although Mother had fallen hard for Daddy, she refused to be pressured into having sex with him before they were married. She was undoubtedly the first woman to ever refuse him, and he didn't like it. He took her home one night after a frustrated attempt to get her into bed and said, "Mary, I'm not coming back. You can wear it out pissing through it, but I'm not coming back if we're not going to have sex." Mother was devastated but adamant. She would not give in.

She cried her eyes out because she really loved him, but she just couldn't bring herself to have sex before marriage. The way she had been brought up simply wouldn't allow her to do it. Plus, she was terrified of getting pregnant. All her life she had been warned she could get pregnant from a toilet seat if she weren't careful, and she wasn't about to take any chances.

But it seems Daddy, too, had fallen hard. He came back and told her, "Okay, I want to marry you—but with one condition: we don't settle down. I want to travel. Let's just go and see the world." Mother was overjoyed and willing to agree with anything he wanted. She would happily follow him wherever he wanted to go.

Shortly after they married, Mother got pregnant with me. I don't imagine Daddy was thrilled. But she kept her word, and barely six months after I was born, on January 24, 1950, we moved to Anchorage, Alaska, which wasn't even a state then. Daddy got a job as a bush pilot, taking people out to hunt bear, moose, and caribou.

We arrived in the evening. Mother held me in her arms as they walked down an unpaved street, both sides lined with saloons—like something out of the Wild West. And just like a scene out of an old western, a man came crashing backward out of a saloon and landed in the street. Mother's heart sank as she hugged her infant daughter and thought, "What have I gotten us into?"

She hated Alaska. It was so cold, and there was always ice and snow everywhere. Daddy was gone most of the time, and I was so little she spent much of her time housebound with me. Mother tried to be a good sport, but she wasn't cut out to live in a cold climate in such a remote part of the world. She gamely went out with Daddy on a hunt one time and got frostbite on her ear. That put a quick end to her outdoor adventures.

She began pressuring Daddy to leave Alaska, and eventually we did, moving first to Washington state and then to Modesto, California. My mother was much happier in both places, and my father was content, too. He was flying, and that's what really mattered to him.

No matter what job Daddy had, airplanes were never far from the picture. We always had either access to a plane or owned our own, so we were able to go places and do things that people normally don't get to do. It seemed the most natural thing in the world to me to hop in a plane and fly somewhere to have dinner or visit friends, and we did that frequently.

When Daddy's father got sick we returned to Oklahoma. After he died of a heart attack, we stayed around for my step-grandmother's sake. My father was restless, though, and eager to try something new. He got the notion he wanted to be a crop duster, though he had never done it before, and Arkansas, which had lots of farmland, seemed like the logical place to try it. His venture was a success, and Arkansas became our permanent home. We lived in a couple of very small towns before settling down for good in Brinkley, about seventy miles east of Little Rock.

All this moving around was an adventure to me. My parents were so positive about every move we made that I couldn't help being excited, too. It never bothered me that I had to leave friends behind, because the most important thing to me was my family. I was the most secure when I was with my mom and dad. It didn't matter where we lived as long as we were together. And I did make friends along the way—some I remember—but it never bothered me to leave them behind, because I always made new friends.

My mother was so good to me. She stayed home with me and was a playmate when I needed one. I never felt a real void by not having longtime friends or relatives nearby. My mother and father were truly the core of my existence. I realized later in life how good our nomadic existence had been for me. Unlike a lot of kids who had never been outside Arkansas, I had seen other people and places and done things they had only dreamed about. I felt it was an advantage for me.

It was in Arkansas that I began my lifelong love affair with singing. I had always enjoyed getting up in front of any kind of audience; I was a natural ham. Mother knew my singing voice was better than average, so she started entering me in talent shows all over the state.

To our surprise, I was winning them. I was comfortable on stage and it must have shown. That easiness combined with my dark hair, light blue eyes, and freckles made an irresistible combination for the judges. I managed to win some of the talent shows without even singing. I took home a sweepstakes award for doing a pantomime of "Sweet Nothings" by Brenda Lee, beating a very talented boy who played the piano and another girl who sang. Then I dropped the pantomime act and started singing myself. I had a strong voice even as a nine-year-old, and I always brought home a trophy of some sort. It gave me a sense of confidence to realize I could affect people's emotions just by singing a song.

I also did a dance party television show in Little Rock called "The Steve Stevens Show." Steve Stevens later introduced me to the head of United Southern Artists Records in Hot Springs, and my professional recording career began. Daddy's nickname for me was "Little Scooter Bill," so I recorded "Lock, Stock and Barrel" under that name. I also recorded "When the Saints Go Marching In" and a song titled "Let's Do The Itch" under the name Geannie Flowers. "The Itch" was a dance Steve's dancers had developed during his show.

I was in the fifth grade when I started to record professionally. That set me apart at school, gave me a sort of celebrity status. As I had also won talent contests and had done a television show, I was treated like a star in my little school. Although, I had lots of friends, there was a little bit of jealousy among some of them, which I suppose was natural. But at such a young age, it was difficult to deal with emotions I didn't understand too well. I just thought some kids hated me, and I couldn't figure out why.

One day I came home from school, upset over something unkind one of the kids had said to me, and my father gave me some advice that I carried with me into my adult life. He said, "Scoot, if you weren't exciting, they wouldn't talk about you. Don't feel bad because you're different and you're out of the ordinary. It's better to be talked about bad than not at all—it's still publicity."

It didn't mean much to me at the time, but later when I was cast into the public spotlight as Bill Clinton's mistress, I remembered that advice. Lots of unflattering things were being said about me, and I thought back often to what Daddy had told me. When things were darkest, I would console myself by repeating his words, telling myself that I was exciting—that's why reporters wrote about me. And just so long as everyone spelled my name right that's all I should care about. It was small consolation, but at times, his advice gave me some badly needed strength.

During the same time that I was first recording, Daddy would take me to bars where I would sing with the band, although I wasn't yet a teenager. I remember visiting Daddy in Shreveport, Louisiana, where he was working, spraying red ants. He took Mother and me to a bar where he had met Jimmy Elledge, who had the hit song, "Funny How Time Slips Away." I got up and sang with the band, wiggling around and having a ball.

I loved singing in bars. A sort of sexual tension seemed to fill the smoky rooms and though I didn't quite know what it was all about, I liked it. I loved being a part of that adult world—so mysterious and alluring. I just knew I was getting an inside glimpse of something I shouldn't be seeing. What kid can resist that?

For a time we lived in Hunter, Arkansas, a little bitty town of less than two hundred people, so small it didn't even have a sheriff. So nothing prevented me from learning to drive as soon as I could pester Daddy to let me. I was driving his truck or his car all over the place by the time I was twelve. Bars and cars—I loved having access to that forbidden, grown-up world.

Brinkley seemed like a giant metropolis compared to Hunter, even though it's population was only about five thousand when we arrived in 1962. I was still singing and making records, but I was starting to get involved with school life, too. I loved being a cheerleader—out in front of people, performing and hamming it up. But, eventually, cheerleading began interfering with my recording. I had to decide between one or the other. A recording career requires dedication, and it wouldn't leave time for much of anything else.

One night I was on the bus with the other cheerleaders, on the way to a game, when my mother stopped the bus and pulled me off. I had to rush off to the recording studio. Everything had come together all at once, the right band, the studio time, and I had to go right then.

I cried all the way to the recording studio and arrived looking sullen and all puffed-up. After the session, my parents sat down with me and said, "Look, unless you want to do it differently, we're going to discontinue all this until you get out of school. If you want to sing professionally then, it'll be up to you. But you can't do both—you can't be a cheerleader *and* have a singing career."

It was an easy decision: I wanted to be a part of the school activities. But looking back, I wish I'd decided differently. I wish my parents had done what many parents do: forced me to be disciplined with the admonition that I would appreciate it later. But they didn't, and the rest is history. I often wonder what would be different now if I hadn't chosen to postpone my singing. If my recording career had been successful, I certainly would have been long gone from Arkansas, and maybe I never would have met Bill Clinton.

Life as a teenager was a blur of activity mixed with a growing awareness of boys. My parents insisted I wait until I was sixteen before I started dating, but I managed to fudge just a little bit and had my first date a month before my sixteenth birthday. It was Christmas time, and we were in Sulphur, Oklahoma, visiting my grandmother. I met a boy who was a freshman in college, and he asked me out. To my surprise, my parents agreed.

We went to a movie and then parked by a lake. He was teaching me the sign language used by the deaf, and everything seemed very innocent. Then, during a lull in the conversation, he lunged at me and started grabbing. I pushed him back and said sharply, "What are you doing?" He replied defensively, "I knew you were too young, you're just a kid." I shot back, "You better take me home," and he did. He was smart enough to know that nobody wanted to mess with my daddy. I knew exactly what he was doing, of course. I just wasn't prepared for it on my first date with someone who was almost a stranger.

I dated around a little bit, but always seemed to be going steady. It was just too complicated to juggle several guys at the same time. It was easier to have a steady boyfriend even if it only lasted a few weeks. My parents kept a watchful eye on me once I started dating and had definite rules concerning my activities. I never considered them harsh, though. In fact, my parents were a little more liberal than some of my friends' parents because they felt they could trust me. But Mother was particular about whom I chose to date. She wanted me going out with only the nice boys from families with money, and if I decided to see someone she didn't approve of, there was hell to pay.

Mother wanted the very best for me. She sent me to charm school when I was fourteen so I would learn to be ladylike and have impeccable manners. She wasn't a social climber in the sense that she wanted to advance her own status in town, but she certainly wanted me to do as well as possible. I didn't resent her plans for me; I knew she wasn't trying to use me for her own purposes. I was her only child and she wanted me to have every opportunity life could provide.

Mother encouraged me to enter beauty pageants while I was in high school. She thought it would be a good experience and that I would gain poise and learn how to handle myself. I even won one of them—some obscure pageant in West Memphis, Arkansas. It wasn't a big deal for me, though. I had already been entertaining people for years, and entering beauty pageants seemed a poor second to singing. Much to Mother's dismay, I quickly lost interest in beauty contests.

While Mother was pursuing her plans for my future, Daddy would be developing political contacts in whatever community we were living in, and he usually ended up being very influential. In Brinkley he was quite active in the Republican party and campaigned for Winthrop Rockefeller for governor. By the time we had been in Brinkley a few years, Daddy owned the airport as well as a couple more airports around the area. Rockefeller kept some of his planes at the airport in Brinkley, and Daddy would frequently fly him around.

Rockefeller owned Petit Jean Mountain, where his house was located, and Daddy would go to Petit Jean for special parties—usually politically oriented. Being a Republican in a small Arkansas town was really bucking the system since Democrats generally ruled. Orville Faubus, a Democrat, had been governor for twelve years, and Daddy was determined to help Rockefeller replace him.

I caught the bug from Daddy and became president of the Young Arkansans for Rockefeller. I was fascinated with the issues and the importance of it all. Faubus had been in power such a long time, but the state was still pitiful. One of the only paved roads in the county was to his house! We held mock elections in our school and provided whatever assistance we could to Rockefeller's campaign.

I enjoyed my small-scale political activism. Through that group I met Winnie Rockefeller, Winthrop's son, and dated him for awhile. Winnie liked me; he called me from England once, which impressed me. I had never had a boy pursue me from that far away. Mother was ecstatic. She kept insisting, "You're going to like him." But I had a boyfriend, Joe Clifton, and I really didn't want to date anyone else. So I would protest, "I don't want to. I have a boyfriend." But Mother was adamant. "You are going to go out with him."

So for Mother's sake, I did go out with him a few times, but I just didn't have an interest in him. I liked Joe. I knew the Rockefellers were wealthy, but when you already have everything, how can you measure more? I couldn't conceive of anybody having more than I had. We had a nice home, nice cars, and nice clothes, and I had no concept of what their millions or billions of dollars actually represented.

Daddy had high hopes for me just as Mother did, but unlike her, he didn't want to engineer success for me. He wanted me to make it for myself. I was Daddy's princess, and he always told me I could do anything I wanted to do. He would say, "Don't be the stewardess; be the pilot. Don't be the nurse; be the doctor. Don't get married until you've done everything else you want to do."

Both my parents had so much strength and self-confidence, I couldn't help inheriting some of it. I refused to accept certain limitations. If I really wanted to do something, nothing was going to get in my way. My parents never wavered in their support and encouragement. They never belittled me or made me feel I couldn't achieve great things. Love radiated from them with such constant force that at times I could almost grab it and hold it to me.

Daddy would have given me the world on a silver platter had I asked. He loved to put his arms around me and paint pictures in my mind of all the grandiose things I was going to do. I'd ask him for money, and he would reply, "How much do you want? I'll give you a pile of money so big you can't hold it." Even as a child I knew he didn't mean it literally; it was just his way of telling me how much he loved me.

Sadly, the unconditional love, trust, and support my parents gave me was often absent from their relationship with one another. Even though they loved each other very much, there was tension between them from time to time because of Daddy's womanizing. I never knew to what degree he was involved with other women, but I do know Mother caught him a few times. She went out of her way to catch him. If she suspected he was with another woman, she hunted for him, and most of the time she caught him. Then things would get very unpleasant in our house.

They were always affectionate toward one another—Daddy would goose Mother or pat her on the butt, and she'd just giggle. And they'd call each other "Honey" or "Darling." But when she caught him with another woman, things got mighty cold around the house.

We attended the Baptist church occasionally but were never strict church-goers. Daddy quoted the Bible, and there was a strong Christian influence in our household, but we didn't make it to church on a regular basis. So when Daddy started to take a serious interest in the church choir, Mother got suspicious. It seems there was a woman in the church choir who was fooling around a little bit with Daddy. My mother started doing her surveillance work, caught them, and put a quick end to it. Once again, the tension at home was so thick you could cut it.

As the years passed, the strain increased. I was fearful they would get divorced, but at times I almost wished they would. My world revolved around my parents; they were my security. But when they were having one verbal confrontation after another, it was unbearable. I was seventeen by the time they actually divorced, and I was torn apart. Other than my mother's battle with cancer years later, that was the most devastating time of my life.

It was a bitter, nasty divorce. Daddy brought a stripper to town from New Orleans, Mother had her investigated, and everyone was dragged into court. They squabbled over every detail of the property settlement. My reaction to all this was, "If this is how it ends, I don't want any part of it." That experience influenced me in my decision to not get married, because I saw this very bitter ending at a young age. I lacked the maturity and insight to put it all into perspective.

Though Mother was strong and self-confident, she always felt insecure about Daddy. She loved him, but simply couldn't put up with his running around. She wanted me on her side and drew me into the battles between them. I adored my father, but I also resented him for what he was doing to my mother, and I was so angry with him. I've realized since then that there are usually two sides to a story. But I never believed Daddy was justified in breaking the vows of his marriage, and Mother was not justified in drawing me into it to the degree that she did. Ultimately, when they divorced, there were words between my father and me, and there were scars that never had a chance to heal. He was killed in a plane crash when I was twenty-three years old, when we were just starting to smooth things over.

At the time of the divorce, I was overly judgmental toward my dad. I didn't realize until later that his life was absolutely coming apart. He loved my mother and he respected her. He just had a weakness for other women. It didn't help that women were so attracted to him, too. He had that John Wayne, James Garner charm, and he loved adventure.

He was a kind, gentle person, but he wouldn't hesitate to throw a punch if he was pushed. He was such a strong figure in my life, and I've never met another man who has been able to provide the kind of emotional support that Daddy gave me. He was generous to a fault, too. Mother and I had a big room filled with racks of clothing, some we never even wore. I had a Buick Riviera when I was fourteen years old and a brand new one when I went to college. But even though he indulged me terribly, I wasn't spoiled. I followed the rules and was a good girl. I worked hard at both my singing and in school because Daddy expected the best from me, and I never wanted to disappoint him.

I've never found a man since who was so giving to me emotionally, without any strings attached. Daddy always told me, "I love you just because." It's never happened that way again.

Two

Bill Clinton wasn't the only man from Arkansas who could charm the pants off a girl. Joe Clifton, my first real sweetheart, was a real charmer too . . . and, oh, those beautiful dark eyes!

Joe's mother was a Farrell, a large family that owned, among other things, a coal mine and a trucking company. My family had been friends with his since we moved to Brinkley. As a kid, I always thought Joe was cute, but by high school, he had grown downright gorgeous. We dated steadily in high school and on into our college years.

After graduating, I had planned on attending World Campus Afloat—a shipboard university where students study as they travel the world. But it was so soon after my parents' divorce that I hated the thought of being so far away from my mother. Joe was headed for the University of Arkansas, and I wasn't anxious to leave him, either. So I chose the U of A. I was still away from Mother, but it was easy to make quick trips home. Later, I learned that Michael Douglas, the actor, was a junior aboard World Campus Afloat the year I would have been a freshman. Who knows what might have happened had I followed through with my original plans and attended the traveling college!

Fayetteville, Arkansas, where the University is located, is in the midst of the Ozark mountains, the prettiest part of the state. Lots of mountains and trees make it one of the most scenic little university towns you'll ever see. Being away from our families and living in a college town was fun for Joe and me, and we made the most of it. Although I loved him, an early marriage wasn't in my plans. A whole, big, unexplored world awaited me out there, and I wanted to see and experience it. I also knew I would probably want to sing again someday. So college life was the perfect environment for me right then. It was a time to play and meet new people.

My new black Buick Riviera was the only one like it on campus, and people came to know me by my car. When I wasn't out cruising the campus, I was often with Joe at his fraternity house getting drunk.

In high school I rarely drank—maybe an occasional glass of wine at home with my parents. I really didn't know much about drinking and didn't like the taste of alcohol at first. My favorite drink was scotch and Coke, because the Coke covered up the taste of the scotch!

In college, however, everyone thought it was great fun to go to a fraternity party and drink until we threw up. It sounds bizarre now because it's such a ridiculous thing to do. But that was what all the "in" people did. I cringe when I remember throwing up in the back seat of some poor guy's car. But back then that wasn't considered abnormal behavior.

Joe and I were having a great time. He was probably more serious about his studies than I was, but he still found plenty of time for me. We loved to head for some private, romantic spot where we could steam up the windows . . . and each other. But my mother had pounded into my head the idea that I had to be a virgin when I got married—and I wanted to be.

Joe wasn't pressuring me to have sex, but he always tried to gently persuade me. Every time we parked somewhere, we came so close to having sex without actually doing it that it was frustrating for both of us. I was torn—I didn't want to get married, but I wanted to be a virgin when I did get married. I also knew that the sexual feelings I was experiencing couldn't be ignored much longer.

The '60s were just ending, and the women's liberation movement was in its early stages. I started hearing things that made sense to me. For instance, women didn't *have* to get married, and they didn't *have* to be married to have sex. So I made a conscious decision that I would have sex with Joe. I knew he'd be overjoyed, and I was so overheated by then I could hardly wait.

It finally happened during a visit we made back to Brinkley. We drove Joe's light green 1967 Impala to one of our favorite spots: the lumber yard. Parked in a dark corner, we could barely wait to get the snaps unsnapping. We moved into the back seat, and as he began to move hungrily against me, I made no move to stop him. Just like in the movies, we made love in the back seat of his Chevy.

Joe told me it was his first time, and looking back on it now, I'm sure he was as green as I was. I remember feeling a little disappointed by the whole experience. The earth didn't move for me like I'd expected it to. Afterward, I thought, "Hmm, is that all there is?" After all those months of building up . . . and then it was over in no time. In fact, I remember thinking the anticipation and the making out were a whole lot more fun than the act itself. Plus, I was really surprised by Joe's reaction. I thought he'd be so happy when we finally did it. Instead, once his hormones cooled down and the guilt took over he said, "You really shouldn't have let me do that." I couldn't believe he would say that, and it made me furious. "Don't put this off on me," I replied angrily. But for years his words echoed in my mind.

He may have felt some guilt about our having sex and not being married, but it certainly didn't stop him from going along with the program. And he never hesitated to initiate sex whenever we had the opportunity. But every time we made love, he would be overcome with guilt and would try to shift the blame to me. Finally, I'd had enough and told him, "The hell with you! What do you mean I shouldn't let you do that? It's my right to do it if I want to." The last time he followed up a session of lovemaking by telling me I shouldn't have let him do it, I settled the issue once and for all. He was still kneeling over me and I reached up and kicked him in the stomach as hard as I could. I said, "Don't you ever say that to me again. Do not *ever* say it again." And he never did.

Unlike Joe, who was pretty focused in college, I followed a rather aimless path, signing up for general education courses without a specific goal in mind. I wish I had gotten more guidance than I did. I had some specific talents that could have been developed with the proper education. For example, I have a knack for interior design. Or I should have concentrated on my music. I had a God-given natural talent in music, but nobody really advised me or directed me to take advantage of it. Even my parents failed to say, "Honey, you need to think about getting a degree in music." Instead, they let me "do my thing," whatever that was, and I'm not sure why. None of my counselors in high school and college looked closely at my test results, which pointed toward certain aptitudes. They were just going through the motions, calling me in and visiting with me for awhile without giving me any sound advice.

Mother told me later that some of my high school teachers and counselors had voiced disapproval of me because I was a privileged little girl driving a big, flashy car while they were struggling to get by on their modest salaries. Daddy's reaction to that was, "Well, I'll tell you what I'll do. I'll buy her a Cadillac Eldorado and put her name in gold on the side. I wonder how they'd like that?" So there was definitely a little resentment there, and I guess it's understandable that they didn't expend a lot of effort to influence my educational direction.

I wasn't mature enough at the time to figure out a direction on my own. I didn't know how to take the initiative, to step back and assess my goals or my talents and then lay out a plan for my future. Plus, I was enjoying my new-found independence too much to spend a lot of time being serious about my life.

After some time at the University of Arkansas in Fayetteville, I decided being a nurse might make sense. So I moved to Little Rock and pursued some of the courses I needed to get the necessary credits, then took a job as a surgical assistant to an oral surgeon for about seven months. What a mistake. One day I came out of surgery covered with blood, looked down at myself and thought, "I always wanted a career with excitement and challenge . . . and this is definitely not it."

After her divorce was final, Mother decided it was time for a change. She left Brinkley and moved to Little Rock to be closer to me. We moved into an apartment together, I started singing again, and the world became an adventure. Singing in bars, being the star of the show, and getting all that attention—I loved it! I had been tied to Joe, to the University of Arkansas, and to my unfortunate stint as a dental assistant, but now it was like the clouds had parted. I was back with my first love, singing. It was 1970; I was young, talented, and had a job that was the equivalent of going to a party every night. Men were paying a lot of attention to me and I was eating it up.

Joe came to Little Rock that summer, after school was out, with the idea that we would pick up where we had left off when I left the university. But I wasn't going for that idea at all. I was willing to go out with Joe, but I wanted to be able to date other men, too. I was meeting dozens of interesting men, having the time of my life, and I wasn't about to go back to an exclusive arrangement with Joe.

I was also getting serious about my singing. My first long-term singing job in Little Rock actually came about as a result of a contact my mother made. She was working for AAA, selling memberships, and a man named Mike Tipton came in. She quickly learned he was part of a popular singing group in Little Rock called The Common Good. They were performing in the Pebbles Lounge at the

Sheraton Hotel, which was the most popular place in town. Actually, every place that was anyplace in the early seventies was busy. There were many live groups singing in bars, unlike today. Cocktail hours were also popular then, with lots of two-for-one specials. It was a high-rolling time. People had money and they enjoyed spending it.

Mike and I formed a quartet called September, focusing on our vocal talents since we were limited in our ability to play instruments. I made a stab at playing a Hammond B-3 organ for awhile, but it wasn't a match. A popular song at the time was "Color My World," by Chicago. During the music break there was a beautiful solo, and almost every time I played it, I'd hit a clunker on that stupid organ, and everyone would groan. They finally took the organ away from me, thank goodness. I never wanted to play an instrument; I wanted to be out in front doing my thing—I wanted to sing!

Our band auditioned at the Sheraton and was hired to split the week with the band that had been there forever, which didn't go over well with them, needless to say. We started with three nights, then we took four. I was earning enough to support myself and I loved it. With a new white Grand Prix, my own apartment, and lots of gorgeous clothes, life couldn't have been better. And having a band in a town the size of Little Rock provided instant celebrity status.

Mike had some disagreements with the rest of us in the group and left, but the band managed to stay together and continued singing in the Pebbles Lounge at the Sheraton. We kept the name September, but eventually it evolved into Gennifer Flowers and September. We had a long stay at the Sheraton, and we also performed outside Little Rock at private parties around the state. I handled all the business affairs for the band: bookings, finances, everything. It didn't take me long to learn the ins and outs of negotiating contracts and maintaining the delicate balance between expenses and income so we'd stay profitable.

Being responsible for the business affairs of the band didn't dampen my desire to have fun. I was dating several men and taking advantage of my youth and energy to cram as much life and adventure into my nights and days as I could. One of my dates was the hotel's food and beverage director, who was twenty years older than I was, but was outgoing and fun-loving. But then he started getting too serious about me and kept threatening to fire the whole band

when I didn't return his feelings. The guys in the band were naturally getting a little nervous about the situation, and so was I. But I
didn't know how to end the relationship without getting fired.

That Christmas, Mother and I visited Oklahoma City, and went
to a club with my cousin and her husband. I joined the band for a song
and, to my delight, they offered me a job. My job status back in Little
Rock was still rocky, and I knew this might be a good opportunity to
slide out of it if things got unmanageable with the food and beverage
manager. Plus, I'd be working in a larger city. Sure enough, when I got
back to Little Rock he got mad at me for something and threatened
to fire the band again. This time I said, "Fine." It was time to move on.

I packed up and headed to Oklahoma City and sang in this elegant, sophisticated private club. I was there for only three months,
but it was an eventful three months. A man named Jim Roderer
swept me off my feet, and we became officially engaged. But the
romance died almost before it began. I may have been turning into
a good businesswoman, but I was still flighty as a hummingbird
when it came to romance.

★ ★ ★ ★

It was during my brief time in Oklahoma City that I lost my
father. After the divorce, he had remarried, and his wife came to
Oklahoma City in 1973 to train to be an airport ground-traffic con-
troller. Daddy came down to visit both of us, and while he was there,
decided to go to North Little Rock to visit friends. During his visit
to Arkansas, he was giving aerobatics instruction to a young man
when something went wrong, and the plane crashed.

I had gone to my fiancé's apartment for dinner that night
before going to the club to sing. My aunt called to tell me about the
accident, and Jim talked to her. He hung up the phone and sat me
down on the couch and gently told me, "Your dad has been in an
airplane accident, and they're not sure if he's okay. Your aunt wants
you to come over to her house immediately."

I remember I wasn't real worried about it at the time. In fact, I
left for my aunt's house thinking this was just another one of Daddy's
mishaps. In the past, I had seen him crash land in his plane and then
crawl out with just a scratch—and the plane would actually be on

fire. I was sure this was another one of those accidents; maybe he was banged up a little, but he'd be okay.

When I got to my aunt's house and she told me he was dead, I couldn't believe it. I wouldn't believe it. It had to be a mistake. His body was cremated, and his ashes were sprinkled over a mountain in Alaska. I never saw him in a casket or saw him put in the ground, and somehow I just couldn't accept that he was gone. He and I had been estranged to some degree since the divorce, but we were just starting to communicate again and to deal with some of those old issues.

As I said earlier, my dad was the only man who had ever loved me unconditionally. His death hit me so hard that I shut it out, I just couldn't deal with the grief. We had a memorial service for him in Oklahoma City, and I didn't cry. Although they were divorced, Mother cried her eyes out as she dealt with her memories, but I just sat there dry-eyed and numb. About two weeks later I was at my cousin's house with my mother, and someone mentioned Daddy's death, and it finally hit me—he really was dead. I would never see him or talk to him again, ever. I started crying and couldn't stop. I was sobbing uncontrollably, from deep down inside. The pain was so strong and I felt so empty and helpless. Finally, Mother had to give me something and put me to bed. Even after that, for a long time, I still kept thinking it wasn't real, and somehow he would walk around the corner and come through the door.

As I've matured, I've come to understand my father better. I still don't condone his womanizing, but I understand him better now as a complete person, and I regret I never had the chance to tell him that. I was so angry with him because of the divorce, and before I was able to completely come to terms with that anger, I lost him. When he died, we had just begun to heal some of the old wounds, but there was still a lot we needed to do and talk about. I know if my dad were alive today, we would thoroughly enjoy each other. He had such an exciting, wonderful personality, I know he would be a hoot to spend time with today.

★   ★   ★   ★

Even though Oklahoma City had a much larger population than Little Rock, there was less going on there. So there I was, twenty-three years old, not much was going on professionally, and my brief engagement had not worked out.

Dallas beckoned. When I had visited there, I saw a lot more opportunity. It didn't take much to persuade me to move. I got to town, rented an apartment, and quickly found a job singing at the Steak and Ale. Almost immediately I realized this had been a good move. I was in a new environment, meeting new people, and I was beginning to accept and deal with my father's untimely death.

Although Mother and Daddy had been divorced several years by then, she took his death very hard. So a fresh start in a new city appealed to her, too, and she followed me to Dallas. And her move paid off in a big way—because that's where she met my future stepfather.

Mother lived in an upstairs apartment, and Jim Hirst lived downstairs. She was a real doll, my mom—blonde, tan, weighed about ninety-five pounds—just adorable. She would go outside to empty the trash, and here would come Jim, offering her a martini. "This guy won't leave me alone," she complained to me. "I can't even go outside without him offering me a drink." I chuckled at the thought and asked, "Well, is he cute?" She thought a minute then smiled, "Yeah, kind of." "Then talk to him," I urged her.

The next thing I knew, they were seeing each other. Mother really liked Jim because he was so stable. He was with Southwestern Bell and later retired after thirty-five years with the company. His personality was similar to my dad's, but they differed radically in that Jim is a straight-ahead guy whereas Daddy was a maverick, constantly taking side paths.

Mother didn't want me to know she was staying the night with Jim occasionally. But one night I went to see her late, around 11:00 p.m. I was wearing five-inch heels and was clomping up the stairs to her apartment, and they heard me from Jim's apartment. Mother knew it was me and whispered frantically to Jim, "Oh, my God, that's Gennifer. Get up. We've got to get up and get dressed. She may come back down here." Jim jumped out of bed, raced around gathering up his clothes, jumped into the bathtub, and closed the shower curtain. He stood there for a minute before he realized there he was, a grown man, holding his clothes, hiding in his own shower!

Meanwhile, Mother quickly dressed and stood by to answer the door. When I didn't get an answer at her place, I thought I might find her at Jim's. So, I clomp, clomp, clomped back down the stairs and knocked on his door. They quickly opened the door and stood there looking like Barney Fife and Thelma Lou from the *Andy Griffith Show*. Their clothes were kind of askew, their hair was sticking out all over the place, and they both had guilty looks on their faces. I said, "What are you two doing?" And they both said sheepishly, "Nothing, nothing." Mother told me to go back upstairs and wait for her there.

The thought had crossed my mind that they might be sleeping together. But that was something I just couldn't picture my mother doing. Not that I would have objected, but it just seemed so out of character for her. It wasn't until years later that Mother and Jim told me the whole story about that evening. Maintaining decorum was important to her, and it was a long time before she could see the humor in it.

While living in Dallas, I sang in two different locations of the Steak and Ale. I also performed at several other places during the year or so I was there. On one occasion, my agent booked my piano player and me in a supper club in Oak Cliff for a week. Gene and I drove out there for work the first night, with him dressed in his tux and me in my long evening gown. We pulled up to this place that looked like a converted drive-in restaurant. First, we drove by it, then turned around, and drove back. I was puzzled, but said, "That's the address. That's it." Gene protested, "It doesn't look like a supper club," but we decided to poke our heads in and take a look.

Well, it was a real dive, full of rednecks. I called my agent and asked if he'd ever been out to this place. "Of course, I've been out there," he said. "You liar, you have not!" I yelled, "They don't want to hear *us*." I was singing "Satin Doll," and they wanted to hear "Please Release Me." It didn't look promising. But the owners of the place said, "Look, we're willing to give it a shot if you are." In that business, you work from week to week; there's not a lot of longevity. Plus, I needed the money. So Gene and I agreed to try it, and things actually worked out okay. The customers were very open-minded and warm-hearted.

Dallas was a lot of fun, but I missed Little Rock. No place had been as comfortable for me as Little Rock and I'd never had it as good anywhere else. I didn't have the guts to move to New York City where I might really make a big splash. To me that place was nothing but a big black hole. I simply wasn't brave enough to venture out that far on my own. So Little Rock was very appealing at that point. I had been a big fish in a small pond there, and I was ready to enjoy that again. I made up my mind to go home.

I couldn't have known that by returning to Little Rock I was throwing myself right in the path of an oncoming freight train named Bill Clinton.

Three

A Freight Train Named Bill

L ittle Rock. Home at last! It was 1975, and I now had enough experience and savvy to know just what to do. I got busy right away and formed a band: Gennifer Flowers and Easy Living. I stopped by the Pebbles Lounge at the Sheraton, where I used to sing, and talked to the man in charge of entertainment. He wanted a new band and said he would love to have me come back, along with my new band.

That pleased me. I couldn't believe it was that easy to regain what I'd left behind when I left Little Rock, and I was looking forward to all the fun I had enjoyed before.

We had a wonderful arrangement at the Sheraton. The hotel had us on sort of a mini-circuit, traveling between Sheratons in Fort Smith and Little Rock. We would work for three weeks, then have a week off, but get paid for four weeks. The money was good and we were having a great time. I was running the band and learning how to handle individual personalities. Initially, if someone got out of line, I would just fire him. Even though I might have been justified in doing so, I soon learned it was much smarter to handle each person differently in order to get the most out of him. I became much better at managing people and keeping everyone happy.

A couple of years after I returned to Little Rock, nightclubs began losing favor as a result of stricter drunk driving laws. As was inevitable in the entertainment business, my time at the Sheraton finally ended, and I was struggling a little to keep my schedule filled. There were still singing jobs to be had, but they were getting tougher to nail down. So when someone approached me about making some commercials for the Hot Air Balloon Theater, I was delighted. It was a nice change from singing and nightclubs and I enjoyed it.

The Hot Air Balloon Theater was a children's theater, so they created two characters—"Miss Heaven Lee" and "Captain Cloud" for the commercials. As it turned out, there was actually a local stripper who went by the name of Heaven Lee, but by the time we found out,

27

it was too late to change my character's name.

Not only were those commercials fun to do, they also brought me to the attention of David Jones, the president of KARK-TV channel four. He saw me in the commercial and contacted my agent to see if I might be interested in coming to work at KARK as a news reporter. I was excited by the prospect, and David assured me that if I showed an aptitude for the business I would rise quickly through the ranks, and the anchorwoman's job would be mine. At the time, women were just beginning to gain access to the anchor desk. Until the early seventies, it had been virtually a men-only occupation, so this would be a chance of a lifetime for me.

This seemed like a perfect opportunity to expand my horizons, and I eagerly accepted the job. I was hoping I could combine television exposure with my singing and travel around making personal appearances. It would certainly be a different approach to my career, and I was game to try.

I had taken a journalism course in high school, and I thought, "How hard could it be?" Not hard at all, as it turned out. I found out early on that I didn't necessarily have to be a skilled writer to do well. I just had to learn how to encapsulate stories in a thirty-second slot, complete with a witty opening and a catchy ending. But that didn't intimidate me. I had been writing my own promotional material for years, and I figured when it came to my on-air style, I could imitate someone I respected, like Jane Pauley, and do just fine.

So I went through the interview process, and David Jones was an elegant, wonderful man—one of the few men I've met who was kind and professional, but didn't try to get in my pants. I felt like he really respected my ability. I can't say the same about Gary Long, the station's news director at the time, however. What a horrible man. He was a ferret-faced, skinny bastard with acne who had a huge chip on his shoulder. My guess is he'd had little luck with women during his life.

He sat in on my interview and didn't impress me. Apparently, he felt the same way about me. When David Jones called me back in, he said, "I'm going to offer you the job, Gennifer, but I want you to know what you're in for. When I asked Gary what he thought about you, how he felt about your interview, he said he thought you were a pretty girl with big tits." I shot back, "Well, he's right about a couple of things, but I also have brains." I told David I really wanted this opportunity, but if I'd only known how miserable Gary would try to make my life, I might not have been so eager.

As it turned out, Gary wasn't the only one who was unhappy with my being part of the team. The whole atmosphere in that newsroom was negative toward women. I don't know about other stations at that time, but the thinking around ours was that women were strictly there for their looks, and they had absolutely nothing to contribute intellectually. To add insult to injury, all the guys in the newsroom were coming on to all the women at the station. It was really a difficult place to work. And I was trying so hard to learn my job because I didn't know much about news reporting.

I remember one man in particular who was extremely hard on me. He was the weekend news anchor, so he was the one in charge on the weekends and he assigned all the stories. He was so mean to me, saying condescending things and putting me down every chance he got. It got so bad that I finally complained. When David Jones confronted him, this man actually admitted that he had been so cruel to me that he'd been having bad dreams about it. And he actually apologized to me.

I did have an ally at KARK though, a fellow reporter named Deborah Mathis. She was very helpful when I first started working there, answering my questions and helping me with stories. Deborah was also one of the women later named as having had an affair with Bill. Whether that was true or not, I never knew. But I remember him telling me I should be careful what I said to her, because she had a big mouth. Maybe what he really meant was she might let on that the two of them had been involved, and he didn't want me to know that.

Deborah was talented, articulate, professional, and very beautiful. She caused a stir around the station in more ways than one, too. For starters, she talked about sex all the time, which made it hard for me. She succeeded in egging on the men, who were all trying to get in the pants of every woman in the newsroom anyway. It was difficult to be taken seriously when the atmosphere was so sexually charged all the time. Plus, as I said, most of the men didn't try to hide the fact that they resented our presence.

My assignment editor actually told me, "It's not like this in other newsrooms, Gennifer. Deborah keeps things stirred up. When you move on, you'll find it easier to cope in this business than you're finding it here."

Another person at the station whom I remember fondly was Tom Bonner, the weatherman. He really went out of his way to help me when the situation became unbearable. He even went to David Jones and tried to defuse things with some of the male reporters, and they did settle down some.

Eventually, Tom became president of the station. He was a diehard Clinton supporter, and when the story broke years later about our affair, he told the press, "It was real unlikely that Gennifer would meet Bill Clinton on a story, because she did feature reporting." That statement had one purpose: to protect Bill Clinton. I was not hired as a feature reporter exclusively. Granted, the stories I covered on Bill were not all hard news. Bill spoke to organizations, he spoke at churches, he cut a ribbon here and there. So I guess those could be considered fluff feature pieces, but I did cover hard news, too. I reported whatever I was sent to cover, and that included a multitude of very boring meetings, some so boring I'd rather have been stabbed in the eye and gotten it over with. But I covered them.

I had been with the station just a few weeks when they sent me to cover a story about Bill Clinton. Although the sun had already set, the air was still warm . . . but I was shivering a little. Not with the anticipation of meeting Bill Clinton, who to me was just some politician, but because I wanted so badly to do a good job, to appear professional and sure of myself. I knew I looked the part—I was wearing my favorite burgundy dress that hung loose in the back and tied in front, and high heels. My hair was long and dark then, and I had it styled up. Little tendrils of hair kept escaping and were blowing around my face in the gentle breeze, but I was too focused on the task ahead of me to care.

I had seen Bill before, but had never met him. I tried to imagine if he would be easy or difficult to question, and I didn't think I'd have too much trouble. The prospect of interviewing a politician didn't unnerve me at all, because at that point I was considered somewhat of a celebrity myself. I had been performing all around Little Rock as a singer and was getting plenty of recognition as a television news reporter, too.

I *was* nervous, but only because I was thinking about how to handle myself and how to present the interview. This was my first assignment out on my own without another reporter along to back me up. There were several other reporters at the airport, too, so when Attorney General Clinton descended the stairway from the plane, I was determined to get his attention. It turned out to be easy. As soon as he heard my voice and turned to look at me, I might as well have been the only reporter there.

When he walked right over to me with a big smile on his face, giving me a seductive once-over and asking "Where did they get you?" I was really irritated. Even though my heart skipped a beat or two, I really just wanted to do my job.

As I headed back to the station, some inner voice told me there was more to Bill's behavior than just a casual flirtation. But that same inner voice neglected to tell me just how serious Bill would soon become.

I saw him often after our first encounter, and he always singled me out and stared at me, as if he were trying to swallow me with his eyes. One day, I was waiting to get a statement from him, standing in the middle of a crowd of reporters. Bill came out of his meeting and, as usual, found me right away. He strolled up to the group, hands in pockets, charming smile already in place, and said to the other re-porters, "Sorry guys, you'll have to wait just a few minutes. You understand." Then he gave me his undivided attention, somehow managing to answer my questions while seducing me with his eyes. The other reporters were left cooling their heels.

When he finally made his move on me, I had such ambivalent feelings. But still, I gave in and let him have my phone number. I struggled with the issues. I knew it wasn't right. He was married! But my resolve melted as soon as he called the next day and asked if he could come see me. I was so attracted to him by then that I let the urge to be with him get the better of me.

As I waited for him to arrive at my apartment, I had such mixed feelings about getting involved with him: I didn't want to be just a casu-al, one-night stand for him . . . and I wasn't entirely sure he wouldn't try to get me into bed the minute he walked through the door. But I really did kind of hope we would end up in bed eventually.

My apartment was so small that in the living room I had only two antique chairs with a little table in between them. So that's where we sat, drinking wine and talking about anything and everything. By the time he left that night, after giving me a sweet kiss goodnight, I knew I was hooked.

Bill really was a master of his game. He knew that walking in the door and immediately trying to jump my bones would be a mistake. I would have thrown him out on his fanny. Instead, he behaved like a perfect gentleman. And the result was I was so eager to see him again, I could hardly wait. Bill wasted no time; he phoned me the next day and we quickly made plans for him to come to my apartment again.

I had barely closed the door behind him before he pulled me into his arms and began kissing me. All that sexual tension that had been relentlessly building for weeks in both of us suddenly erupted. A desire far beyond a physical attraction overwhelmed me. Everything about this man excited me: his brains, his charm, and his incredible sexuality.

We stumbled toward the bedroom, ripping off our clothes as we went, reluctant to release each other long enough to step out of them. My apartment may have been small, but my bed was built for a king. It took up most of the room: an imposing four-poster canopy draped with luxurious fabrics and buried in soft, sensuous pillows. But it could have been an army cot for all we cared. We collapsed onto it and eventually covered every square inch of it.

As a lover, Bill was great! Though not particularly well endowed, his desire to please was astounding. He was determined to satisfy me, and, boy, did he! At times I thought my head would explode with the pleasure. This was more than just great sex, it was great everything. I was falling in love with Bill Clinton, inside and out. On this magnificent night, there were no thoughts of "Is that all there is?"

On the contrary! We spent two or three hours together, mostly making love. During our short breathers, he would hold me and stroke my hair. He was so sweet and tender. It was as if I were the only one who existed for him at that moment. Nothing else mattered: not Hillary, not his responsibilities, nothing. He focused on me just as I focused on him. It was beyond my power to do otherwise. This man made me want to give back what he was giving, and what he was giving was sensational.

By the end of the evening, we were both drenched with sweat and my hair was a wet, tangled mess. But he just laughed and held me tighter, assuring me that I looked perfect. He convinced me it didn't matter how I looked; he was as consumed with me as I was with him.

His stamina amazed me. We made love over and over that night, and he never seemed to run out of energy. Had he stayed with me the entire night, I have no doubt he could have kept going 'til dawn. But spending the night was out of the question: Bill had a wife to go home to. I wanted him to stay so badly, but because I felt so happy and content, I was eager to make it easy for him. As he left, I urged him to be careful. I wanted him to come back, and I certainly didn't want to cast a dark cloud over our blossoming affair by making impossible demands.

After he left, I spent a restless but happy night. I had just had the greatest sex of my life with the most remarkable man I had ever met. He left his undershirt for me to hold through the night so that I could keep his scent close to me even after he was gone. I was floating on a cloud and had no desire to come down.

My assignments often included covering stories involving Bill. To my great delight, I saw him the day after our love-filled night together. When I heard that I would be reporting on a speech he was to give, memories of the night before set my body tingling. The thought of seeing him again after our passionate first night together made my knees weak.

I arrived at the hall where he was to speak and stood in the back with my cameraman. The stage was dominated by a large podium, with chairs on either side of it. Bill was seated very near the front of the room. He spotted me almost as soon as I entered—he seemed to be looking for me. Even though he was sitting in front and I was standing in back, he turned around to look at me—our eyes locking in silent acknowledgment of the passion we had shared the night before. The problem was that he kept looking back at me so often that other people were turning around to see what he was looking at. Bill was the speaker and the center of attention, so wherever he looked, everyone else looked, too!

To my relief, he finally stood to make his speech, which successfully drew his attention away from me. When he finished speaking, I had no trouble cornering him to get a statement. It was hard to keep a straight face and ask him serious questions when all I could think about was how his hands felt as they caressed my naked skin. It was difficult for him, too. He couldn't keep the smile off his face and was having trouble concentrating on what he was saying. Unmistakable sexual vibes were passing back and forth between us.

Somehow, though, we both managed to play our parts, and I made a beeline for the telephone as soon as we finished the interview.

I was in the phone booth calling the station when Bill came over and tried to crawl in the booth with me. I was excited but horrified and I hissed, "Bill, there are people standing around here. This is crazy." He kind of grinned and said, "I don't care." I shot back frantically, "Well, I do. I've got a job to do here." "I've got to see you again," he pleaded. So I told him to call me later in the newsroom.

He did call later and I took the call at my desk in the newsroom, which was crawling with people. But I didn't care. Hearing his voice was more important than anything else right then. We got so involved in the conversation that Gary Long, the news director, snapped at me to get off the phone. I didn't want to hang up, and we kept talking. Gary was giving me nasty looks and finally made it clear that if I didn't end the conversation my job would be at stake.

During the first few months of the affair, our passion and desire for one another was so consuming that we met whenever our schedules would allow—as often as two or three times a week. It was easier for him then, before he was elected governor, because he didn't have security guards around him all the time. He could come to my apartment or meet me at a hotel without too much fuss.

Although I still occasionally had qualms about our involvement, it became easier each time I saw him. I didn't try to justify it. I knew it wasn't a good idea, but I really felt that any guilt should be on his part. I wasn't married; he was. Words like adultery and fornication came to mind, but I shut them out. What was building between us was too good to be spoiled by recriminations. I did feel guilty later when his daughter, Chelsea, was born. But when it was just Bill and Hillary, it didn't bother me as much as it probably should have.

Four

Getting to know Bill was an adventure. He was intelligent and dynamic and so driven to succeed. But at the same time he had a soft side. He couldn't hide his passion for politics and he loved to discuss his favorite issues when we were together. Then two minutes later he would be tenderly making love to me. Every facet of his personality, from his sense of humor to his drive for politics to his gentle demeanor with me, was thoroughly captivating. I was grateful my job gave me an excuse to see him so often in a professional capacity. I felt it broadened my understanding of him as a total person. Seeing him in public so frequently also added to the danger that we both relished. How far could we go without getting caught?

During this time, he called me at the station frequently. Deborah Mathis and I had desks very close to one another, so she often was nearby when he called. I tried to keep my voice low because I knew our affair had to be kept under wraps, but there was so little privacy, and she could tell I was talking to someone special. She finally got the information out of me: the man I was so doe-eyed over was none other than our own attorney general. At the beginning of our affair, Deborah was one of the few people who actually knew Bill and I were seeing each other. Bill and I tried hard to keep our relationship as quiet as possible, but it was difficult to keep it entirely to ourselves.

Both of us had instantly recognizable faces, which made it impossible for us to be seen in public together. But I was singing occasionally at the Camelot Inn in Little Rock, and sometimes Bill would come in to hear me, alone or with a group of friends. One evening, he came in and sat at a table with several friends. The mood was sultry, and the lounge was softly hazy with cigarette smoke. As soon as I saw him, I changed my program and substituted a love song, "Since I Fell for You," which I sang directly to him. Then I sang the song he had told me reminded him of me: "Here You Come Again."

I joined his table during a break, pretending to be a casual acquaintance. When Bill got up to make a telephone call, one of the women in his party leaned over to me and whispered, "He couldn't take his eyes off you while you were singing." Even though I had sung to him intentionally, throwing caution to the wind, her comment almost made me wet my pants. Every time something like that happened, I would get nervous. It didn't seem to faze Bill, though. He was casual about his behavior and never seemed to care that we could get caught.

My mother, on the other hand, was anything but casual when she found out I was seeing a married man. She was staying with me in Little Rock shortly after Bill and I first got involved. He called one night and she answered the phone. She could tell by my side of the conversation that this man meant something special to me, so she questioned me about him when I hung up. When she heard he was married she hit the roof. With her, it was much more than just a religious or moral principal; she had been married for many years to a chronic womanizer, and it had caused her tremendous pain. She couldn't understand how I could even think about getting involved in that type of situation. She was right, of course, and I was wrong. Had I listened to her, my life would likely be completely different today. But I didn't.

We had a huge argument about it and she threatened to go see Bill and even to talk to Hillary if I didn't put an end to the relationship. Even though I was twenty-seven years old and thought I was all grown up, I knew my mother would do what she threatened. But I couldn't stop seeing him, so instead, I stopped talking to her about it. We never mentioned it again, although Bill actually called me at her home once when I was visiting, and she answered the phone. She knew who it was and it started another argument, but I was able to convince her not to worry about it.

Years later, when the story started to come out and Bill denied it all, my mother stood behind me one hundred percent. Even though she felt all along that what Bill and I did was wrong, she knew that it was true . . . she had suspected for years that I had continued seeing him because I never became attached to any other man. So she hated it when people questioned the truth of my story.

★　★　★　★

During my stint at KARK, I substituted frequently on an

FYI-type guest-interview show. One of my guests was a woman who headed an abortion clinic in Little Rock, and the topic of abortion made for quite a controversial interview. Never afraid of controversy, I dug right in and explored both sides of the issue, not dreaming for a minute that I was sitting there at that moment pregnant with Bill Clinton's baby.

Within a couple of weeks of that interview, in the middle of December 1977, I got a little worried because my period was late. So I quickly called my doctor and made an appointment. Even though I had my suspicions, I was still unprepared when he confirmed I was indeed pregnant. I sat there for a moment after he told me, in stunned silence. I had been using a diaphragm for birth control, but really hated it. It was so clumsy, and more often than not I'd accidentally pop it toward the ceiling when I tried to use it. Bill told me he didn't think he could have children since he and Hillary had been married almost two years and she hadn't gotten pregnant. So I got careless and didn't use the diaphragm as often as I should have, and sure enough, I got pregnant.

I was horrified. No way was I ready for a child, but this was *Bill's* child, so I had mixed emotions about it. I went through the whole thought process of what we might produce together and that maybe this would be a catalyst for him to leave Hillary. These were dangerous thoughts, I knew. As much as my heart wanted to believe he might leave her for me, my mind told me otherwise. Bill had a definite political agenda, and she was a key player in his plans. I knew she was smart and that she was a hard-driving force behind him. Because of that, she was valuable to him, and he knew he needed her to get what he wanted.

What Bill wanted right then was the governorship of Arkansas. The 1978 gubernatorial election was coming up fast, and he was going to have to make a public announcement about his intentions. He had already confided in me that he was definitely going to run, but nothing had been made public yet.

All these things were going through my mind as I wrestled with a decision. I decided to wait and see what Bill's reaction would be before I made up my mind. He came over to my apartment one night shortly after I got the news, and we sat side by side in the same chairs we had sat in the first time he came to see me. I didn't beat around the bush; I told him immediately that I was pregnant.

I watched his face carefully to see his reaction. He was surprised, of course, but he didn't seem stricken or scared. The first words out of his mouth were, "Are you okay?" I burst into tears. I was so relieved he was concerned for me and not angry or accusing. But at the same time, I was scared, unsure of what was going to happen. He took my hand and asked how I felt. "Awful! The smell of almost everything makes me sick to my stomach, and my whole body feels puffy and sore."

I made small talk, deliberately stretching the conversation out to give him time to say what I so desperately wanted to hear. All he had to do was give me the slightest indication he would leave Hillary and marry me, and I would have said yes in an instant. But the minutes were passing, and the words I was waiting for never came. What he said was comforting, but what he didn't say broke my heart. His concern for me was sincere and I was grateful. But his silence told me everything I needed to know . . . there would be nothing coming from him beyond concern.

Having a child without a husband was out of the question for me. I made up my mind on the spot. I told him right then and there I intended to have an abortion. His face still showed nothing but caring concern, but I'm sure he was inordinately relieved. He never said a word about keeping the child or even wondered what it might be like if things were different. He was sweet and supportive, but it was very clear that marrying me was the furthest thing from his mind.

Bill gave me some money for the abortion, and I called the woman I had interviewed on TV. She helped me maintain some privacy when I went to the clinic. What a traumatic experience: painful both physically and emotionally. I felt like I had been deceived, too. Bill had assured me he couldn't have children, and I didn't know for sure if he was sincere. I reasoned that maybe he really believed he couldn't and that this was just an unhappy accident, but it still planted a seed of doubt.

The day of the abortion, I drove myself to the clinic. I had hesitated to confide in anyone because I feared that the word might get out about Bill and me. As soon as I opened the door of the clinic, the medicinal smells hit me. The room was colorless and without personality, and a large seating area with sparse decor held only some chairs and a few tables for magazines. I joined the other women sitting and waiting to be called. As I watched them I wondered about their stories. There was a pretty, dark-haired young woman with a deep tan sitting next to a frumpy-looking housewife type. No matter how they looked, or how they ended up here, we all had this one thing in common. We were about to take a painful step.

The clinic did group counseling sessions right before the procedure. We all sat listening and cooperating with the counselor, but as I looked at the faces of the women in my group, I wondered if they were feeling the same conflicting emotions that I was.

The abortion itself was painful, and there was nothing to ease the pain. The procedure is demeaning: the poor woman lies flat on her back, legs up in those hateful stirrups with an impersonal tool ready to enter her body and remove something very personal. After it was over, I went in and sat in a chair and sobbed—partly from physical pain, partly because I felt totally devastated. Since then, I've wondered how well a man could endure such an experience.

I had the abortion in the afternoon, and Bill called me shortly after I got home to find out how I was doing. I didn't reassure him; I was uncomfortable and very upset. But I was touched by his concern. As soon as I recovered, I got serious about birth control. Since diaphragms only work if you use them, I switched to birth control pills and never missed a one. I never ever wanted to go through that experience again.

As emotionally difficult as that whole situation was, I had no intention of ending our relationship. I was in love—temporarily insane! Even though hope was dim and fading that he might leave Hillary for a life together with me, I had no desire to see anyone else. Not that the opportunity didn't present itself.

I was still singing here and there, doing some private parties. It was getting me out, and I was seeing people, which seemed to satisfy my need for a social life. In my mind, nobody could begin to compare with Bill. You know that old saying, "thirty minutes of wonderful is better than a lifetime of okay." So I was willing to accept our relationship on that basis and enjoy it for all it was worth. It was terrific, thrilling, and I wanted it to stay that way as long as possible.

Bill was starting to make noises about running for governor. This caught the attention of KARK, and they sent me out to get a statement from him at an event where he was speaking. I already knew he was definitely going to run, but I also knew he wasn't ready to announce it yet. The station wanted me to really put him on the spot, to say to him, "Tell the truth: are you or are you not?" The news director was insistent. "Get this from him!" My heart sank. How was I going to do this? I had a cameraman with me, and I knew I wouldn't have much chance to forewarn Bill.

I waited until he wrapped up his speech, and I cornered him. That wasn't hard. He was more than willing to be cornered by me. The cameraman was behind me, so I looked Bill in the eye apologetically, and said under my breath, "I've got to ask you this." Then I asked him if he intended to run for governor. I had no idea how he would respond but wasn't expecting his reaction. He couldn't help smiling, but he dished out some double-talk and evaded my question! Bill Clinton was already perfecting the tools he would need to be a successful politician. I didn't push him as I would have with someone else. I let it go for his sake.

During this time, Hillary was never allowed to occupy my thoughts for very long. I knew if I let her image creep into my relationship with Bill, a shadow would be cast over our otherwise happy times together. I had never seen her in person—or even a picture of her—until I attended a function in Russellville, Arkansas. Colleagues had told me she wasn't particularly attractive and had a real Yankee attitude, which put people off. I was curious about her, but ambivalent about actually seeing her face to face. The Russellville function was a political fund-raiser, and I knew Bill would be attending. It never occurred to me that Hillary might be there, too.

I went to the fund-raiser with a friend and was having a wonderful time chatting with the other guests and catching Bill's eye as often as I could. I wandered over to the bar to get a fresh drink, and while the bartender was pouring and mixing, I glanced across the room and there stood Hillary less than five feet from me. Someone standing near me confirmed that's who it was.

I was shocked. She looked like a fat frump with her hair hanging down kind of curly and wavy. She had big, thick glasses; an ugly dress; and a big, fat butt. My first thought was, "What in the hell does he see in her?" I knew Bill was capable of loving a woman for her mind, but I couldn't understand what I was seeing. Besides looking dumpy, she was behaving oddly—flamboyantly buzzing around with a drink in her hand talking and laughing. She seemed intent on trying to draw attention to herself, and she certainly was doing that.

Everyone was staring at her, wondering exactly what she was up to. All I could see was this fat butt wiggling around. I kept looking at her, and I thought, "What is she doing?"

Seeing her there brought home a few realities, though. Knowing about Bill's wife was one thing, but seeing her in the flesh was another. It angered me. At the time I really wanted him to leave her, and I thought, "Why? Why is he with her?" He was so cute and smart, and she was so unappealing. Surely her brains didn't offset her looks.

I do think Hillary looks good now . . . better than she's ever looked. I think she had a lot of help with her appearance during the presidential campaign, and it really paid off. But back then it made no sense to me that Bill could have married her in the first place.

Speaking of Hillary's looks . . . a funny thing happened to me at a hotel gift shop in Los Angeles in 1992. I picked up a few items to buy and when I went to the counter to pay, the woman asked me, "You know who you look like?" I figured she was going to say Gennifer Flowers, but she said, "Are you Hillary Clinton?" I was flabbergasted. I said no and looked her right in the face to see if she was teasing, and she wasn't. I signed my name and room number to the ticket and left. I wondered if she looked at my name after I left and thought "Oh, my God. I can't believe I'm telling his mistress that she looks like his wife." Believe it or not, I've been mistaken for Hillary more than once. I think people make a connection between the two of us, but they mix up the faces. At least I hope that's the explanation for it.

Bill and I didn't talk about Hillary much. Every once in awhile he would be exasperated with her over something, and he would complain about her cold nature. He called her "The Sarge" or "Hilla the Hun." But occasionally he would speak respectfully of her, too. He really admired her and the things she tried to accomplish, but I think a lot of times he was put off by her hardness.

The time Bill and I had together was too precious to waste talking about his wife, but when I heard some rumors floating around Little Rock, I had to speak up. He was with me at home one evening, and I cautiously told him, "There's something you need to know. I've been hearing tales around town that Hillary is having a thing with another *woman.*" I watched his face to see his reaction, and couldn't believe it when he burst out laughing. I was stunned! I asked him what was so funny. "Honey," he said, "she's probably eaten more pussy than I have."

Bill said he had known for a long time that Hillary was attracted to women, and it didn't really bother him anymore. His first clue came from her lack of enjoyment of sex with him. He said she was very cold and not playful at all in bed. She didn't like to experiment and insisted on the missionary position and nothing else. Because she wasn't enjoying herself, neither was he. Sex with her became a duty, nothing more.

Their marriage was not a happy one, although he never came right out and said it. He didn't have to. The signs were clear. He was with me, after all, telling me he loved me and seeing me every chance he could. Even though I knew he wasn't happy with her, he never gave me the impression he intended to do anything about it. During the first several months of our affair, we would engage in bedroom talk to the effect of "If we could only be together . . ." or "When we're together . . ." But he never came right out and said, "I want to get a divorce," and I never asked him to. I look back now and wonder if he actually wanted me to ask him to get a divorce. Would that have made the difference?

Just about anything Bill did was okay with me. I wasn't about to criticize him for fear of creating distance between us. So when he casually put his hand in his pants pocket and pulled out a joint one night, I was startled but kept silent. I thought how foolish it was of him to carry marijuana around, but it was typical of his bulletproof attitude. He felt comfortable enough to continue smoking marijuana occasionally when he was with me. I didn't object. I didn't like it and was glad when he finally quit using it around me, but I never voiced any disapproval other than the fact that I had no intention of smoking it with him. By the way, he most certainly *did* inhale.

I never saw him use cocaine, but he talked about it. He complained about how cocaine really had a bad effect on him. It didn't stop him from using it, though. He told me about a party he had been to, and said, "I got so fucked up on cocaine at that party." He said it made his scalp itch, and he felt conspicuous because he was talking with people who were not aware drugs were at the party, and all he wanted to do was scratch his head. He was afraid if he continued to walk around scratching his head, people would think something more serious than dandruff was going on with him.

I tried cocaine a few times and didn't like it. What *is* the big deal? It reminded me of going to the dentist. It made my eyes and sinuses swell and I looked like a frog. I just didn't understand what people saw in this drug.

I don't think Bill used cocaine often, but there were several occasions when he mentioned to me he had gotten high on coke. I wondered if he worried about using drugs when he was such a high-profile person. But just as he thought he was bulletproof in his relationship with me, that same reckless attitude extended to his drug use. He seemed to think nothing could ever touch him in an adverse way.

I stayed with KARK for just about a year and finally decided I had had enough of all the harassment and tension in the newsroom. I sent some audition tapes to a New Orleans station and to the NBC affiliate in Atlanta and got a positive response from both, which helped convince me that I had accomplished something in that business and could move on if I wanted. I thought long and hard about it and came to the conclusion that if I were going to be in a back-stabbing business, it might as well be the one I knew best: the entertainment business.

About that time, an agent who had seen me perform in Tulsa contacted a local talent/booking agent to see if I'd be interested in auditioning for country entertainer Roy Clark as a back-up singer. I didn't like country music and wasn't really infatuated with the idea, but my agent told me this would give me the chance to meet a lot of people who could help my career. Jim Halsey was Roy's manager and he had built quite an agency. The Jim Halsey Agency represented acts like The Oakridge Boys, Tammy Wynette, Don Williams and lots of other top-name acts. So being part of that organization was a big deal. That appealed to me. I had spent the last year working myself to death to gain some respect at KARK without much success. I was ready for some positive moves, so I did the audition.

What an experience. I had been told I would get a private audition with the band, so a girlfriend and I got in the car and drove to Tulsa. We found the hotel and went to the ballroom where the audition was to be held. When we walked into the room I was shocked to see several hundred other girls waiting for their turn. Needless to say I was not happy. I told my girlfriend, "Forget this. Let's just head back to Little Rock." But she convinced me to stay, just to see what it was like. So I took a number and waited with the others. I did, however, waylay the music director and make it clear to him that I had been told this would be a private audition. He apologized for the mix-up and begged me to stay and give it a shot.

It took quite awhile to get through all those auditions. They finally moved the last group of us into a small banquet room to wait our turn. I was getting real bored, so I got a beer and sat with my friend until they called me to sing. I remember I sang "We're All Alone," a Boz Scaggs' song that Rita Coolidge had made popular. I could tell right off that the music director liked me, and I felt the same way about him. They narrowed the group down to six and had us come back to sing our songs again. Then they chose two of us.

I have to admit I was thrilled to be chosen from such a large group, and once I visited the Jim Halsey Agency in Tulsa, I was real impressed with the level of professionalism. Plus, I could practically smell money when I walked into his office. He had it decorated with lots of Indian art, and pictures of all his stars hung on the walls. All of a sudden, I began to feel pretty special.

The only sour note in my excitement was that I had to move to Tulsa, Oklahoma, where Roy was based. I dreaded the thought of leaving Bill, but I needed to go forward. I knew it would probably be better for him if I wasn't around during his 1978 campaign for governor. Before I left the TV station, our sportscaster, Rob Wiley, took a leave of absence to work on Bill's campaign. One night he took a call that came into campaign headquarters, and the caller angrily said, "You better tell Bill Clinton we know about his affair with Gennifer Flowers, and it better stop." Rob turned to Bill, who was there, and told him what the woman had just said. Bill's pretty quick on the uptake, and he replied, "I'm just flattered that anyone would think Gennifer Flowers would have an affair with me."

Bill told me about the phone call, and it made me a little uneasy. I felt we were getting much too close to exposure. It didn't seem to bother him a bit, though. But the time was right for me to leave. He was disappointed I was leaving town, of course, but he encouraged me to pursue my career. I told him, "I feel like I really have never gone as far as I could professionally. I haven't tried New York or LA. Although I've performed in other places, I haven't really pursued a career nation-wide. I need to do this." He was sad, but said "I think you should; I don't blame you. I want you to do it if that's what you want."

It was tough to leave, and I cried halfway to my new home. I loved Bill so much, and even though I wanted to follow this path, the reality of leaving him nearly broke my heart. As I drove down the highway, putting more and more miles between us, I wasn't certain I would ever see him again. But, as it turned out, I had underestimated his tenacity.

Five

Performing with the Roy Clark show was quite an experience. I loved it . . . but I wouldn't want to do it again. I had never traveled in such high caliber entertainment circles before. These folks were true professionals, and they drew the audiences to prove it. I had been on lots of stages and sung before plenty of large groups, but to walk out onto a stage and sing in front of 35,000 people—that's a real thrill. It's also a little scary. Roy was so popular with his fans—he had just won country music's "Entertainer of the Year" award for the second time—and there was never any barricade between the stage and all those thousands of screaming, cheering people. A few security guards were all that stood between the crowd and us.

That enthusiasm didn't stop at the stage, either. When we'd roll into town in the bus—which is the way we traveled most of the time—the fans would close in. Fortunately, the bus had shades, because if we arrived at concert sites with the shades up, fans could see through the windows and would go wild. We felt like monkeys in a cage at the zoo. The fans didn't realize Roy was almost never with us on the bus—he flew in on his private plane and would arrive at the actual concert site quietly. We had to go through some elaborate methods of getting off the bus because the fans always seemed to be waiting to swarm over us. I had no illusions that I was the star of this show—the only star was Roy Clark. But just being part of the show lent me a sort of rub-off celebrity status, and I enjoyed it.

A short time on the road and we had become a fairly tight group. Moving around from town to town meant the only friendships I could form were within the show—these were the only people I had regular contact with. We had a road band of five guys who traveled with us, three back-up singers, and Roy joined us occasionally.

Roy was a big-hearted guy and very good to the back-up singers, but he had a major cocaine habit, and he drank a lot—every day. He also, surprisingly, was quite a womanizer. He had a wife, who wasn't on the road with him all the time; a girlfriend on the television show *Hee Haw*; another girlfriend in Las Vegas; and on top of all that, he became involved with one of the other back-up singers.

Roy was known to have sudden temper tantrums. He'd be all coked up or drunk, and he'd throw glasses against the wall. His personality could change in an instant. One minute he was happy and calm, the next he'd be screaming and yelling. Despite his temperament, though, he was always ready to party. If a party wasn't happening, Roy would make one. And he didn't like to party alone. He always insisted everyone stay with him until he was ready to call it a night.

I discovered the hard way what happened to those who tried to sneak out early. We were performing in Lake Tahoe, and after the show Roy had a party in his dressing room. The room was fairly large, but people were coming and going all night, so it stayed crowded. Cigarette smoke filled the whole area, and after several hours of partying, the atmosphere was oppressive. By five in the morning I was tired. I didn't use cocaine, didn't feel like drinking anymore, and just wanted to go to my room and get to bed.

Roy was in a back room doing his cocaine when I stood up and announced I was going to my room. The door burst open and he shouted, "If you leave, you're fired!" That was too much. I have a bit of a temper myself, and I said, "Listen, if you want to fire me, go right ahead. But nothing you can threaten me with is going to keep me in this room." Roy's eyes got big, he went back into his little room and slammed the door, and I left. He actually apologized the next day, and I felt I had achieved a minor victory.

Like I said earlier, I never liked using cocaine. And, boy, am I thankful I didn't, because I sure had every opportunity to use it—day and night. Little bowls of cocaine were set out like appetizers at every party.

The wildest parties took place when we were playing in Las Vegas or Lake Tahoe. It would be easy to blame the ever-present supply of cocaine on the road band; road bands have a reputation as hard partyers who have a free-flowing supply of drugs. But when we were in Vegas or Tahoe, the road band wasn't usually with us. Roy would use the orchestra provided by the hotel where we were performing. So it was up to him to keep himself supplied with cocaine, and he always managed to stay well stocked.

Roy eventually cleaned up his act. When I worked with him

again several years later at his theater in Branson, he had quit drinking and doing drugs—I think his doctor told him to clean up or die—and he was doing much better. I give a lot of the credit for his recovery to his wife, Barbara. She stood by him through so many shenanigans: drinking, drugs, other women. She was a rock of support when he needed it most. And he combined that support with his own inner strength and made a remarkable turnaround. I have a lot of respect for what Roy accomplished with his personal life as well as his career.

When the show would roll into Las Vegas, it was exciting and a relief at the same time. We'd actually get to stay put for a few weeks, and it gave me a chance to meet a lot of stars, including Bob Hope. Lots of performers who were in Las Vegas at the same time we were would stop by Roy's dressing room. One man I found particularly fascinating was Evel Knievel. He was in town planning another of his famous stunts. A homing device would be implanted in his stomach, and he would jump from an airplane into a haystack. Find the Knievel in the haystack. The deal never came together, but at the time I met him he was actively promoting it.

He was a pompous ass, totally obsessed with himself and his "achievements." And he loved showing off his diamonds. Everything out of his mouth was me, me, me; I, I, I. "I did this; nobody else can do that." Just an idiot. But in spite of that mouth, and all his scars and broken bones, I found him physically attractive. I was getting bored with our routine—finish the show and go home by 3:00 or 4:00 a.m.; sleep; get up and eat; and it's time to go back to work. So, when he asked me to have a drink with him, I thought it might be an adventure.

We went to a bar at the Circus Circus casino and almost immediately got into a confrontation with a girl who was photographing him for a magazine article. At some point during her assignment she must have developed a personal interest in Evel. She was not pleased to see him with me, and made no attempt to hide her displeasure. We had a few drinks, but she kept hovering around sending me looks that could kill. Add that unpleasant scene to the mindless worship he demanded and got everywhere we went, and I was ready to call it a night. But he would have none of that, and we ended up at his room, and this moonstruck young woman had actually left him a rose in front of his door. And I thought, "Well, this ought to be good, if she's chasing him this hard." And it was!

Evel called me several times after that evening, asking me to come to Palm Beach to join him. If my schedule had been different, I might have considered it, but it was fun to tell him no and prick a little hole in that great big ego of his.

Life on the road with the Roy Clark Show was grueling. We crisscrossed the United States and Europe with only short breaks, then we would return to Tulsa. It was as if our road schedule had been determined by someone throwing darts at a map—back and forth across the country we would go. It was difficult to see Bill during this time because I was gone so often. But occasionally I would have some time off, and he would come to Tulsa to meet me, or I would go to Little Rock to see him. We kept in touch frequently by telephone, though. It was easy to reach him at his office in the Capitol Building or at the governor's mansion. The chain of command was familiar with my name and I would always be put right through to him.

I hadn't seen Bill for several weeks, but I knew he was due to come to Tulsa for a political function. He called to tell me he was on his way, and I waited for him anxiously. I was missing him badly and looked forward to a few sweet hours together. When he arrived he had the best surprise for me—he told me he was going to spend the whole night with me. I had always hoped we would have the chance to stay together all night, but I never believed it would happen. We occasionally took short naps together after making love, and there was something so special and satisfying about being able to snuggle up close to him and doze off. Bill would turn on his side and draw his legs up, and I would put my arms around him and curl up behind him—"getting in his crook" I called it.

That night together was a rare treat. I lay awake for hours, watching him sleep and counting his breaths. I was surprised when he started to snore gently. I wasn't surprised that he snored, only that I had never heard it before.

I was never happy when Bill had to leave me, but I had gotten used to his leaving after a few hours. Watching him walk out my door after a whole night together was a different story. It really pounded home how much he meant to me, how rare and special our time together was. It was excruciating to watch him leave, and it left me feeling empty and alone.

One of my goals in leaving Little Rock was to put our relationship in perspective and create some emotional distance between us. After our night together, I felt I had taken a step backward. But I was still determined to weaken our connection if I could. Although I still held a tiny flicker of hope for a future with him, in my heart I knew it wasn't likely to happen.

I redoubled my efforts to concentrate on my job and to explore relationships with other people. While on the road, I went out occasionally and I often made new friends, and the Roy Clark Show was like a great big family. I felt I was beginning to develop a life beyond Bill. But in spite of my good intentions, I still never hesitated to see him whenever I had the opportunity.

After nearly a year with the show, I was exhausted from being on the road. Even worse, I had gained weight because we never ate on schedule. We ate when we had the chance, not when we were hungry. A lot of our meals were in greasy-spoon restaurants just off the highway, and sometimes I would find myself eating hamburgers and french fries at three o'clock in the morning. I rarely had a chance to get any exercise, and the pounds started to pile up.

The novelty of traveling and performing all over the United States and Europe had worn off. It had become such a grind—get on the bus, go into a place, get a room, change for the show, do the show, get on the bus, go to the next city, get a room, shower, change for the show, do the show, get back on the bus. We did a stretch like that for almost two weeks once without a break! I was just miserable. I'd find myself looking out the bus window at the neighborhoods we drove through thinking, "I wonder what regular, real people are doing today? I wonder what their lives are like?" Because my life had become surreal, I longed for a return to normal, a chance to put my feet back on the ground.

I began to plan what I would do next. I had relatives in Dallas and had lived there before. Plus, I knew the market there was still good for my business. So I headed straight for Dallas, found an apartment, and started from square one again, which is the way you have to do it in the entertainment business.

Naturally, I thought seriously about going back to Little Rock to be near Bill—he was a strong pull. But after my year apart from him, I knew I needed to maintain the distance between us to get him out of my system . . . as much as I could, anyway. Furthermore, I had gone about as far professionally as I could in Little Rock. In order to continue advancing, I needed to be in a larger city with more opportunities.

By this time my résumé was impressive, and I had no trouble finding work in a Dallas club. As soon as I was hired, I assembled some musicians and we were ready. I stayed in Dallas just a short time, though, before I was offered a job in Fort Worth, singing at a new restaurant called Remington's. The owners wanted me to do some public relations for them, as well. This was too good to pass up. I moved to Fort Worth, did public relations during the day, and sang four nights a week. Before long I also became the interim manager of the restaurant.

I was happy with my responsibilities at Remington's, but the restaurant was on shaky ground. It was a popular place, but the owners were having financial difficulties with some of their other concerns and didn't pump enough money into the restaurant to keep it going. It stayed open only about six months . . . but what a six months!

During that time, I thought I was making progress in distancing myself from Bill, but it was hard to resist calling him every once in awhile, and he called me, too. Music had always played a part in our relationship, and whenever I performed certain songs, they always brought back memories. I'd always have music playing when he'd come to my apartment. We both loved the Commodores—"I'm Easy" and "Three Times a Lady" were special favorites. We'd also listen to Frank Sinatra, the Chairman of the Board. Bill liked Steely Dan, and Kenny Loggins was someone we listened to a lot. For my part, songs like "Wedding Bell Blues" and "Don't Mess with Bill" had a habit of playing over and over in my mind during our early years together.

While I was singing at Remington's one night, I was surprised to see Bill come in. He was in Dallas for a conference, and he had made his way to Fort Worth to see me. It had been months since we had seen each other. All the memories came rushing back in an instant. I pictured myself in his arms and could hear him telling me he loved me as he had so often. He listened to me sing for a bit, and as I sang I could feel the passion rising to the surface. There he was with his piercing eyes, staring at me in that familiar way. Not only was I powerless to resist him, I had no desire to resist him.

He took the key to my apartment and said he'd wait for me there. But before he left I introduced him to a dear friend from Fort

Worth: Jay Wallace. He told me later how impressed he was with Bill's class and charm. I couldn't have agreed with him more. I rushed home to him, and melted into his arms. Nothing had changed between us. All the love and passion we had shared in Little Rock was back in an instant. It had never really diminished; I had just tried to pretend it had. We were still a perfect fit, mentally and sexually. We had missed each other terribly, and it showed in the intensity of our lovemaking. Later that night, as I lay in bed stroking his hair, I knew that he was deeply rooted in my heart. I could move to Dallas, or California, or to the moon for that matter. But distance wasn't going to get Bill Clinton out of my system.

Even though Dallas and Fort Worth weren't his home turf, we still had to be careful about being seen together. All the southern states are close together, and the governors' names are well known. Had Bill sat in the bar at Remington's for very long, the manager and some of the regulars were bound to join him and start a conversation. And unless he gave them a phony name, there would have been some questions about why the governor of Arkansas was spending the evening in a bar watching Gennifer Flowers. So we were forced to be just as discreet in Fort Worth as we were in Little Rock. But we were used to it by this time, so it didn't seem like a big deal. It was a small price to pay to be able to snatch a few hours with the man I loved.

When Bill wasn't right in front of me, casting a spell over me, I really believed I could develop an interest in someone else. I knew the only thing that would tear me away from him would be to fall in love with another man. But it had been nearly three years since I had fallen in love with him, and so far I hadn't met anyone who was his equal. But I kept looking.

Fort Worth was similar to Little Rock in that it was easy to be a big duck in a little puddle. A newspaper reporter had written an article about me titled, "Gennifer with a 'G,' Class with a 'C.'" The article couldn't have been more flattering—it complimented my singing ability and called me the most eligible bachelorette in town. I loved the attention I was getting. Men were asking me out, and I decided to take advantage of the opportunity to shift my focus away from Bill.

I was dating one of the owners of the restaurant who was separated from his wife and going through a rather nasty divorce. Not an ideal situation, but at least he was legally separated. His son lived with him, and we would get together every once in awhile at his apartment. I liked him a lot and thought there might be a chance for a future with him. Maybe he was the one who could divert me from Bill. Unfortunately, his wife was unable to let go. Their five-year-old daughter was living with her, and she would call him at all hours of the night saying, "Your daughter is having bad dreams; she wants her daddy." And he would rush off every time she beckoned.

She followed us when we were out together, too. I was trying to be patient, because I still thought if we could get his wife settled down, things might develop for us. But we were starved for some privacy. So one night he told me, "I'll get a room at the Hilton, and when you're finished singing we'll have a late dinner and be able to spend some time together." That was fine with me. I was ready to get serious about this man, and the chance to have an evening alone without being pestered by his wife was appealing.

We had dinner and a few drinks, then went back to the room. Things were just starting to heat up when the phone rang. I heard him protest, "No, no, now don't come up here." His wife had seen both our cars at the hotel and told the bellman she had a sick child; she had to get in touch with her husband. The bellman told her what room we were in!

By this point I had changed into a long negligee, and I panicked! I grabbed my bag, stuffed my nightgown into my underwear, and threw on my fur coat. I told him, "I don't want any part of this. I'm getting out of here." As I tore down the hall toward the stairs and was just opening the exit door, she came off the elevator and headed for her husband, letting out a blood-curdling scream and sinking her fingernails into his face.

I flew down the stairs as fast as I could, but came up short when I found that they ended at the mezzanine. There was no way to get out of the hotel without descending a long, winding staircase that led smack into the lobby. I was trying to walk down those stairs with some dignity, and my nightgown kept falling out from under my coat. I felt like a bad version of Scarlett O'Hara. I finally got to the bottom, raced through the lobby, and ran outside to my car, only to find she had pulled in behind my car and blocked me in. I ran back inside and demanded the desk clerk get me a cab. He pointed to the telephone and said, "You've got to call one." Great. In a panic, I called a cab, but knew I couldn't stay in the lobby in case she came back down. She was a bona fide lunatic and I had no idea what she might do.

I moved back outside and planted myself in a little alcove in the building, looking like a madwoman myself—hair sticking out everywhere, silk gown hanging down under my coat, and a panicked look in my eyes. I tried my best to become part of the wall, hoping that if she came out, she might not see me. Meanwhile, people were walking by, staring at me, and I kept thinking, "Yep, it's me, Gennifer with a 'G,' Class with a 'C.'" Finally, my cab arrived and I got out of there. The next day I told him I wouldn't see him again. I needed another relationship with built-in problems like I needed a hole in the head! So much for my attempt to get Bill Clinton out of my system.

In the meantime, Remington's closed, and I started looking around for work again. I called a friend from Dallas, Kay Hammond, and she told me she was dating a fellow who was going to be singing at the Fairmont Hotel in Dallas, and he was looking for a female partner. The Fairmont! That was the crème de la crème in my business. His name was Robert Phillips, and I went to his home in the exclusive University Park area of Dallas to meet him. He was divorced and had a luxurious house decorated with chandeliers and animal skins, including mink-covered pillows on his couch. It was the ultimate bachelor pad.

He had a set-up in his living room so he could play music with the voices dubbed out. I sang a couple of songs for him, and he liked what he heard. We talked for awhile and liked each other almost immediately. I was thrilled when he asked me to join him in the Pyramid Room at the Fairmont, and I made plans to move back to Dallas right away.

Robert was a sophisticated, nice-looking man with light colored eyes and dark hair. He looked a little like the singer Vic Damone. In addition to being a talented singer, he was a good businessman. I felt fortunate to have lucked into that deal and was glad my background had prepared me for it. Most singers had to perform around Dallas for years before they could get to the Pyramid Room, and I managed to walk right into it. I quickly brushed up on the old standards like "Satin Doll," and I was ready to go.

Singing in the Pyramid Room was one of the highlights of my professional career. The room itself was beautiful—elegantly decorated and set up so it was easy for me to interact with the members of Dallas society that frequented the room. It was the "in" spot at the time. In addition to the Pyramid Room, the Fairmont had the Venetian Room, which brought in big-time talent. The Pyramid became a hang-out for the celebrities when they were between shows or looking for a place to unwind after their show. It was fun seeing well-known faces come in often, and most of the time I was able to meet them. This was my room and I was the star there. It was exciting to meet celebrities like Jack Jones, Nancy Wilson, Harvey Korman, Tina Turner, and many, many others.

Rich Little was appearing at Fair Park in Dallas and came into the Pyramid one evening with friends to have a drink. He was with a date, but slyly invited me to join his table during a break. His date left the table for a few minutes, and Rich asked if he could call me. He was nice looking and obviously very funny, so I gave him my phone number. The next evening he picked me up in a limo with his manager and the now well-known TV personality, Charlie Rose. We went to dinner at one of Dallas' most elegant restaurants, Jean-Claude's.

Rich was charming and hilarious, even without his impressions. We went to the Loew's Anatol penthouse, where he was staying while in town, and it was gorgeous. It had a bathtub so huge my whole bathroom could have fit into it. The room reportedly cost $1500 a night.

I liked Rich and went out with him a few times, and later did an interview with him while I was briefly working for a radio station in Little Rock. I remember a touching confession he made on they way to dinner one night. He told me other entertainers are identified by their singing or acting ability, but half the time he didn't know "who the hell" he was; he was always someone else.

He also told me a funny story about his first appearance on the *Ed Sullivan Show*. Knowing this could be a big break for his career, Rich had been practicing for days on the routine he'd done the night Ed had seen him in the club where he was performing. The night of the show, Ed came backstage to greet him. Rich impersonated that great Sullivan voice as he told me that Ed said to him: "I'm real glad you're on my show tonight, but I'd like to give you some advice. I saw you at the club the other night, and I wouldn't do that routine if I were you."

★ ★ ★ ★

Every now and then, Bill would come to Dallas on political business, and he always saw me when he did. There was no denying that the magic was still there, and my attempts to find someone else had gone nowhere. I began to visit Little Rock frequently to see him. I would make a reservation at a hotel, and Bill would reimburse me later in cash. Once the Excelsior Hotel was built, I stayed there exclusively. It was easy for Bill to find a reason to be there—many conventions were held there, and there always seemed to be something political going on there. So he could be seen at that hotel without raising any eyebrows.

It frustrated both of us not to be able to go out in public together. Even though we treasured the time we were able to spend together, we longed to do things others couples in love do—like going out for a drink and sharing a romantic candlelight dinner. Even the simplest pleasures were denied us—movies, clubs, theater— even a hand-in-hand walk through a park was out of the question.

So Bill tried to get a little creative. He called me from Little Rock one day to tell me he was coming to Dallas, and he asked me to dress up like a man and meet him at the Mockingbird Hilton so we could sit in the bar and have a drink together. "What about my hair?" I asked. "Pull it up under a man's hat and put on a man's suit," he responded. The idea was intriguing, and I considered it. I wouldn't use any makeup, and wearing a man's suit might be fun!

But the more I thought about it, the more I realized what a dangerous idea it was. I'm only five-foot-two, for heaven's sake; I didn't have a man's suit hanging in my closet, or a man's hat; what would I do about shoes? And I have large breasts. There's no way I could disguise that! I couldn't imagine anyone believing I was a man. So we didn't do it. But I did think the idea was a hoot. It would have been interesting to see if we could pull it off.

On one of Bill's trips to Dallas he had some devastating news: Hillary was pregnant. I didn't want to hear this news. I thought back to the child we had conceived together and felt a stab of pain in my heart. Why was he so happy about this baby? Why hadn't he felt that way when I got pregnant? But he was thrilled with Hillary's pregnancy; he considered it a godsend. I was happy for him because he was happy, but I resented him having a child with this woman whom he found it so easy to cheat on.

His eyes glowed with pleasure when he told me. Obviously it never occurred to him that I might be disturbed by his news, but I was. That put the lid on it for me. If I had still entertained even the slightest hope that we might have a future together, the notion disappeared forever that day. It was right there in black and white. So I took my emotional lumps and made a conscious decision to be more open-minded about getting on with my life. I had dated other men and had tried to get serious about a few of them, but I always held something back.

I don't blame Bill for all of my hesitation about getting involved. I know my parents' divorce still weighed heavily on my mind and made me reluctant to commit to any man. But Bill did play a big role. If I met a man and found out he wasn't perfect, I knew I already had someone who was: Bill Clinton. He was always happy to see me and, in fact, went out of his way to see me. When things would get the least bit rocky with another man, I knew I had this little place to run to that was extremely fulfilling, both psychologically and physically. He was my secret haven, my feel-good place.

Although I didn't end our relationship when Hillary got pregnant, I made a mental shift. As far as Bill was concerned, everything was the same and he fully intended to keep seeing me. On the surface, our relationship didn't change. I still loved him, but I also knew I had to pay attention to what I needed. I wasn't sure exactly what that was, but until I figured it out, I intended to just relax and have fun. I had always been a free spirit who liked to have fun, but now I intended to really pursue it.

I quit looking for someone who satisfied me as much as Bill and decided to simply enjoy the different men I did go out with. I didn't need to "bond" with every man I dated—I just wanted to play and not get serious. Bill could still be my "someone special." Once I mentally erased the complications from our relationship, it made it easier to be with him knowing we had no future together.

I had a wonderful job in the Pyramid Room that gave me the opportunity to meet lots of interesting people, and I decided not to hold back any longer. I would go out whenever I wanted, and, who knows? Maybe I'd actually meet someone someday who would steal my heart away from Bill.

So that's what I did. I didn't meet anyone particularly special, but I had a lot of fun. And while I was still singing at the Pyramid, I met a man who offered to help get me a job at the Cipango Club in Dallas. The Cipango was a prestigious private club, and I would make even more important contacts there than I had at the Pyramid.

I was ready for a change. As much as I enjoyed singing at the Pyramid, the Cipango held a special allure for me. I had gone there once when I was just twenty-one and was so impressed with the place that I stole an ashtray to keep as a souvenir of my evening there. To go back there as a singer was like a dream come true!

My job at the Cipango went beyond just singing, which was fine with me. I was always eager to expand my talents. I was hired as a membership director and sang on weekends. It was something new for me, and I tackled it with enthusiasm. I really enjoyed the change of pace but was glad I still had the opportunity to sing, too.

The Cipango was absolutely beautiful inside—lots of wood paneling and exquisitely decorated. One thing about the Cipango—you knew you'd really made it there when the patrons urged you to get up on the bar and dance. It took awhile for me to work up my courage, but I finally agreed one especially busy weekend night. The bar was crowded, I had been singing all night, and was enjoying a break while the band played background music.

I'd had a few drinks or I doubt if I ever would have done it. But some of my favorite members were there that night, I was a little tipsy, and we were all having a wonderful time. Finally someone yelled, "Gennifer, it's time for you to get up on that bar and dance." I didn't hesitate for a second. I climbed right on up, high heels and all, and danced through two complete songs. Everyone was applauding and egging me on, and I was in heaven.

I felt like I was surrounded by a great big family. The members were so nice to me, and several of the other entertainers had become close friends. I was very happy at the Cipango.

But it, too, began to run its course. It was a heavy schedule working during the week as membership director and as a singer on weekends. When I was offered an engagement at another private club in

Dallas, I thought long and hard about it. The Cipango had been good to me, but sometimes my instincts tell me when it's time to move on, and for some reason, I felt the time was right.

The booking at the new club was a one-month engagement with a three-month booking guaranteed after Christmas. That was considered reasonably long-term in my business! So I decided it offered me the security of a steady job that I needed as well as the excitement of moving to a new place and meeting new people.

The first month of my booking worked out great. I liked the new club and was enjoying the new surroundings. But then the unforeseen happened. The ownership changed, and my return booking was canceled. It was late in the year and much too late to secure a new engagement, and I was left hanging in the wind.

I looked around Dallas a little bit, putting out feelers to see if anything was available, but I wasn't having much luck. There was no immediate crisis because I had a little money saved, but I knew I would go through it quickly if I didn't find something soon. It was getting close to Christmas, so I made the only decision I could think of at the moment.

I decided to visit my mother and stepdad for a few days and plan my next move. Muzzy and Pappa, as I like to call them, had married and were living near Branson, Missouri. So while I was there I drove over to Branson and stopped by the Roy Clark Theater.

At the time of my visit, Branson was a small town of about twenty-five hundred during the off season. It doesn't have an off season now, but in the mid-eighties the season lasted about six months. While visiting Roy Clark's theater, I met the manager, and he asked me to audition. I did, and he offered me a job for that season. It seemed like a good solution to my problem. Plus, it would be nice to be near my parents for awhile.

There was nothing sophisticated about Branson, and it really didn't appeal to me much, but I stuck it out for the season. I worked seven days a week for five and a half months. It was a brutal pace.

The entertainment in Branson is absolutely wholesome—family entertainment with women in high-necked collars. I would look out over the audience and see acres of white hair. These were God-fearing folks and they demanded their entertainment be clean. Roger Miller, bless his heart, was performing one night and inadvertently said "shit." He was telling a joke, and the word "shit" happened to be in it. It was a funny joke, too! But the audience went wild. They stormed the office of the management demanding that Roger apologize, be kicked out, get beheaded, and on and on. You'd have thought he slapped their mothers!

I had planned to go back to Dallas after the season ended in Branson. But I had been talking to Bill, and he was trying to persuade me to come back to Little Rock. After my season of hell in Branson, big-city Dallas sounded exhausting. I liked the idea of getting back to a smaller place with a slower pace. I was ready to go home, and I missed Bill, too. I needed to be touched and held by someone who knew me inside and out. I needed Bill to work his magic and recharge me again—I needed a "Bill fix." Without too much thought, I jumped right back into the tempest with no idea just how stormy it was going to get.

Six

It was the mid-'80s when I returned to Little Rock. My relationship with Bill Clinton had endured more than eight years, and in all that time I had yet to meet any man who affected me the way he did. As I drove past the city limits of Little Rock, my feelings were mixed. I anticipated that the intensity of our romance would once again be as strong as it had been during our first months together, and I relished that thought. But by deliberately moving back to the same city as Bill, was I eliminating the possibility of ever falling in love with another man? "Stop it!" I admonished myself. My decision was already made, and there was no sense clouding up my mind with questions that had no answers.

Bill suggested I rent a place at the Quapaw Tower apartment building. "I go there anyway, because I have aides who live in the building," he told me. "It's not far from the governor's mansion, so why don't you check it out?" The Quapaw was a brick high-rise that was modern and comfortable, and I liked the fact it was so close to Bill, too—just a few blocks away! I chose a unit I liked and moved in, with the anticipation of seeing Bill often.

We hadn't seen each other the entire five and a half months I was in Branson. Working seven days a week, I just couldn't get away. So before I was even settled into my new apartment, Bill arranged a reunion. Amidst the chaos and confusion of unpacked boxes and suitcases, we explored the new setting for my four-poster bed. Our physical hunger for each other hadn't been satisfied in a long time. I was starved for him, and we made love as if it were our first time. It was wonderful to have him in my arms again. The long days and nights in Branson faded away, and I truly felt like I was where I belonged.

As we lay in bed with Bill's head on my shoulder, I let my mind wander into areas of thought I usually tried to avoid. I wondered how he reconciled our relationship in his mind. I had certainly struggled with a multitude of issues over the years—his marriage, my pregnancy, Hillary's pregnancy, the clandestine nature of our meetings—did he wage an inner battle, too? We never talked about it, but I couldn't believe he never seriously thought about what we were doing. Bill is a sensitive, caring man, and as unhappy as he might have been in his marriage, I knew he wouldn't want to cause Hillary pain.

Something happened one night that made me think he really did worry about it. He came to my apartment, and, as usual, we sat on the couch and talked for awhile, then started kissing and playing with each other as we moved toward the bedroom. We crawled in bed and were just beginning to make love when he suddenly jumped out of bed and backed up against the wall, shaking and crying. I was horrified. "Tell me what's wrong," I pleaded, but he wouldn't say. He couldn't talk at all, nor could he stop crying.

I was terrified something awful was wrong, but I couldn't reach him. I put my arms around him and tried to reassure him, but he still was shaking terribly. I very gently said to him, "Bill, Darling, it's just me. Talk to me. Tell me what's going on." He wouldn't speak. After a few minutes the shaking subsided, and he weakly said that everything was okay. I persisted in trying to draw him out, to find out what on earth had upset him so, but he simply couldn't talk about it. And I never learned what it was that had affected him so. I was completely confused and puzzled. What could have made him act that way?

The only thing I could imagine was maybe he finally had experienced some feelings of guilt about what he was doing and was overwhelmed by those feelings. Maybe he had made an effort to be faithful to Hillary, just couldn't do it, and was distraught by his weakness. As much as he cared for me, he *was* cheating, and that had to bother him every once in awhile.

It broke my heart to think he was so torn up inside and unable to talk about it. Maybe he had come face to face with a part of him he didn't like to acknowledge: his weakness and desire for someone other than his wife. Whatever it was, he got over it within a few minutes and came back to bed with me, ready and eager for oral sex.

The time we spent together was never often enough nor long enough. For that reason, I think both of us were reluctant to squander even one precious moment by stirring up worry and doubt about the right or wrong of our relationship. Those were things we would have to deal with on our own.

★ ★ ★ ★

Once I returned to Arkansas, Bill came to my new apartment as often as he could slip away—we had so much lost time to make up! He was stopping by three or four times a week. Our relationship heated up again quickly, and the passion was more intense than ever.

But Bill was careless, and the rumors started flying almost as soon as I returned. He would walk right in the front door of the building and take the elevator to the second floor, where I lived. He didn't realize the security guard in the lobby was watching to see where the elevator stopped. The guard knew none of Bill's aides lived on the second floor, and the gossip spread quickly. It got back to Bill, and he called me, concerned. Not concerned enough to quit seeing me, but enough to want to be more discreet. We had to come up with a plan. I told him I would prop the side exit door open with a newspaper when I knew he was coming, and he could slip in and walk up two short flights of stairs without being seen.

From then on that's what we did. But people were catching on anyway. The security guard would walk around the building and see Bill coming in through the side door, and the guard had a real loose tongue. Also, Bill couldn't travel alone any longer; he always had a security contingent with him. While he and I were in bed making love, his driver would be waiting for him downstairs!

Bill loved to jog in the morning, and it was an easy way to get out of the mansion without arousing suspicions. He would jog just over a mile to my place, spend a half hour or so making love to me, then have his driver drop him off a block or two from the mansion, and he would jog the rest of the way. Then he would show up at home properly out of breath. I liked to joke with him that after running all the way to my place he wouldn't have the energy to make love; he gladly proved me wrong again and again.

He had a regular jogging route he liked to follow to my place. From the governor's mansion on Center Street he would turn a few corners until he ended up on Spring Street, which ran behind the Quapaw Tower. My apartment's balcony faced Spring Street, and

63

when I knew he was on his way, I'd wait on the balcony until I could spot him. Then I would run downstairs and prop open the side door. We had our system down pat and continued using it for a long time.

I loved standing on that balcony watching for him. I always recognized him immediately, and it would make my heart jump just watching him run toward me. I was so turned on I could hardly wait for him to get to the door.

Being with Bill again energized me. I was eager to find a singing engagement, but while I was looking for places to sing I took an interim job as a deejay for a radio station. I worked on both the AM and the FM side. An interesting job, but it didn't pay well. Plus, I missed having the face-to-face contact with my audience, and I was anxious to sing again. Luckily, I soon landed a singing job at the Capitol Club, which was an exclusive private city club perched atop the Worthen Bank Building, one of the tallest building in Little Rock. The club was a classy place with a fun-loving membership—perfect for me.

Shortly after I started singing there, the club held a Democratic fund-raiser, and my band provided the entertainment for the evening. When we took a break, Bill McCuen, the secretary of state, cornered me and started putting the moves on me. When Bill Clinton walked in and saw us, he hurried over and stood on the other side of me. Bill McCuen was known to chase women, so Bill Clinton wasn't about to leave me alone with him. It was amusing, because McCuen and Clinton were actually political rivals, and I don't think there was much love lost on either side. So we were all chit-chatting, talking about the horse races, and Bill McCuen said he would send me some passes. Then, without any warning, in walked Hillary.

The room was packed with people, they were literally elbow to elbow, and getting through the crowd was difficult. But she spotted us and made her way right on over. She stood in front of me, no more than two feet away, with an ice-cold look on her face, and politely said hello to her husband. Then she swept her gaze past me and said hello to Bill McCuen, pretending I wasn't there. I didn't expect her to act as if I were her long-lost friend, but there was an awkward silence after she said hello to the men and then ignored me. I was thinking, "Oh, boy. Is this it? Is Hillary going to blow the lid off Bill's and my affair right in front of all these people?" It made the hairs on the back of my neck stand up.

She looked much better than the first time I saw her. Her hair was fixed up and she was wearing a classy-looking business suit. The intensity of her look was real disconcerting and I wanted Bill to do something, but I didn't know what. Panic overtook me for a moment. I didn't know if we were going to have a confrontation or not. I couldn't imagine Hillary making a scene in front of all those people who were so important to her, because she was pretty conscious of her position, but you never know. For all I knew, she might even pop me one on the nose. If the roles had been reversed, that's what I would have been tempted to do to her.

It's funny looking back, but I really had mixed emotions at the time. Here was Hillary staking claim to her territory, which she had every right to do, and part of me wished she would just do it . . . take him with her right then. Well, she tried, but he wouldn't go. She reached up and grabbed his lapel, pulled him down to her and kissed him on the cheek. Then, after what seemed like an eternity, she said to Bill, "I'm going over to the bar for a drink. Would you like to go with me?" Then my feelings changed and I thought, "You son of a bitch, you better not desert me!" He looked at Hillary, smiled, and said, "I'll be over there later. You go ahead." It was a showdown, and I had won—at least that round.

I was so relieved when she walked away that I reached back and grabbed his butt and gave it a good, hard squeeze. It wasn't a romantic squeeze though, more like a "God, I can't believe that just happened" and a "Thanks for staying—I love you" squeeze.

Then I heard a chuckle and looked around to see my guitar player standing behind us watching me put this death grip on Bill's butt. Bill hardly flinched. He just stood there with a look on his face that told me everything was under control. I think he was actually enjoying the moment!

Bill McCuen stood there bemused, with a look on his face that asked, "Did I miss something?" I shook my head in disbelief, and went back up onstage to sing. Bill and I spent the rest of the evening making eyes at each other, like we often would do. Hillary walked by me a couple of times but refused to make eye contact. As far as she was concerned I didn't exist.

Bill and I had talked about whether she knew about us, and although we assumed she did, we never really knew for sure. After that night there was no doubt—Hillary knew.

She and I had another close encounter one chilly fall day at the governor's mansion. Bill and Hillary were hosting a pre-football game party, and Bill arranged for me to bring my band and provide the entertainment.

The governor's mansion! It was a place I'd had dreams and fantasies about. The thought of being where the man I loved lived gave me chills. It also saddened me a bit, though, to know that his wife and child shared that home with him. Would I feel guilty performing there? By putting myself right onto Hillary's turf was I flirting with World War III? I made my decision to enter that danger zone when Bill's secretary called me to make the arrangements.

What a memorable day for me. The party was held outdoors on the beautifully landscaped grounds of the mansion. A grassy incline that flattened out at the top formed a perfect natural stage where my band and I performed. From our vantage point on the hill, we were able to look out over the crowd as we sang. It was a cool day, but the crowd was oblivious to the chill in the air, too excited anticipating a Razorback victory to notice.

The band and I were all set up and performing before I saw Hillary or Bill. She never came near the stage, just wandered around the crowd, greeting people and talking. Bill, on the other hand, spent all afternoon playing his sexy, stare-down game—eating me up with his eyes. As I sang, I watched him talking with different people, and all the time he would be staring at me. The other person would literally be talking to the side of Bill's head. Every once in awhile Bill would turn and acknowledge that, yes, there was a person speaking to him, but for the most part, he or she might as well have been talking to a wall. The whole thing was a real turn-on for me, and apparently it had the same effect on him.

The band broke for a few minutes, and I headed for the mansion to use the ladies' room. It was such a great day! The exhilaration of the crowd was contagious, and I couldn't help smiling as I strolled along. This was about as close as Bill and I could get to being in public together, and I was enjoying myself thoroughly. I brushed my hair back from my face, breathed in the crisp air, and scanned the crowd, trying to spot Bill. Out of the corner of my eye I saw someone walking down the narrow sidewalk right toward me. Oh, my God! It was Hillary!

Whenever I performed at functions like that, the host or hostess usually cordially acknowledged me, saying, "We appreciate your being here. I hope you're comfortable. Let me know if there's anything I can do." Somehow I didn't think Hillary would be quite that genial, and my heart was racing, wondering just what she would do. As she got closer, I mentally steeled myself for the tongue-lashing I fully expected her to unleash on me. But she passed me by without even a glance, passing no more than a foot from me, so close I could smell her perfume as we nearly brushed against each other. She kept her eyes straight ahead—not a word, not a look.

I didn't know what to think. Thank goodness she didn't force a confrontation, but her turning an absolute blind eye to the situation puzzled me. My reaction wasn't quite what I expected. I didn't feel angry, insulted, or embarrassed by her deliberate brush-off. She could have slapped me right off the sidewalk and I would have deserved it. I actually sympathized with her. After all, her husband, the governor of the state, had been eyeballing me all afternoon, and any idiot could have seen it. She had to be furious. Whatever my opinions about Hillary might be, I certainly couldn't argue that my having an affair with her husband should endear me to her. Once again, though, I wondered why she tolerated it.

I went on into the mansion and found the rest room. As I came out of the ladies' room, Bill was waiting for me. Our little visual foreplay over the heads of the crowd had managed to get us both steamed up. He grabbed me around the waist and pulled me to him. Then he started kissing me as if we were standing naked in my bedroom, his hand wrapped in my hair, holding my lips against his. He tried his best to get me to go into the men's room with him so we could release that tension we'd both built up. He held me close and I could feel him, warm and hard, straining against me. The danger of the situation added fuel to the flames we were creating. He took my arms and was leading me toward the door to the bathroom, but I roused myself and listened to my inner voice. My close encounter with Hillary had unnerved me, so I put him off, saying, "Hillary could walk in here any minute and see us together." So could anyone else for that matter; it was a miracle no one else came into the building or out of the ladies room while we stood there wrapped around each other.

Bill didn't care. He was persistent and was convinced we could pull it off. His wife and his constituents were just a few feet away, and he was willing to take the risk. The courting of danger was part of both of our personalities, that love of risk and excitement. But on that day, something told me, "Don't do it, Gennifer." He was being too reckless, and one of us had to behave responsibly. Those warning voices were too strong to ignore. I told him I would be missed if I didn't rejoin the band right away, and I was sure people would be looking for him, too. I pushed him away, headed out the door, and made my way quickly to the bandstand.

It's amazing that Bill and I were never actually caught red-handed, but he seemed to have everything under control. Many people knew of our relationship—his security people, his aides, my friends—but no one seemed too disturbed by it. This was Arkansas, and Bill was king. He had a network of "good ol' boys" that would go to great lengths to protect him. Furthermore, no one really seemed to care that he was cheating on his wife, including Hillary herself.

I was always more concerned with appearances than Bill. Most of the time he didn't seem worried about getting caught, but I tried to be very careful. But one time I couldn't resist sending him home with blatant evidence that he'd been with another woman. We'd established a certain good-bye ritual after our lovemaking. Because he's more than a foot taller than I am, I'd walk him to the door, then climb up onto a chair to wrap my arms around his neck and kiss him good-bye. On this particular night, I had combed my hair and put on lipstick as usual, climbed up on the chair, threw my arms around him . . . and planted my lipstick-covered lips right smack on the back of his collar. I don't know what possessed me, but I did it intentionally. Maybe the thought of Bill leaving me to go home to Hillary was just too much that night. And it wasn't just a smear, it was a perfect, bright red imprint of my lips.

He had no idea what I'd done until he got home and Hillary saw it. He told me later that she demanded to know where the lipstick mark came from, and he brushed it off by saying, "You know women are always hugging me." And she let it go. I was surprised he wasn't mad at me for my deliberate indiscretion; on the contrary, he thought it was funny, and the next day and we both had a good laugh about it. I don't think I would have been as tolerant as Hillary. Had he been *my* husband and come home with a lipstick smooch on his collar, I would have pinned him to the wall.

Hillary, however, never tried to put a stop to my relationship with Bill. In fact, he told me that after he hung up from talking with me one night, she walked into the room and asked, "How's Gennifer?" He looked at her carefully and replied, "Just fine." And that was the end of it. She must have had her reasons for putting up with Bill's infidelity, but it was a mystery to me at the time. In retrospect, I can see that Bill and Hillary's political future was undoubtedly more important to her than her husband's faithfulness. But back then I couldn't imagine why she would close her eyes to his fooling around.

I also think they most likely had some type of agreement about extramarital activities. She didn't ask what he did and he didn't ask what she did. It's obvious the woman isn't stupid, and she's certainly not the type to play doormat. So there must have been a pre-arranged understanding that they would each look the other way. Bill's sexual misadventures have been hinted at for quite awhile and are becoming more known all the time. But now word is circulating that Hillary isn't above reproach in this area either. In the last couple of years, stories have circulated about her reported affairs with people like Vince Foster and possibly Webb Hubbell.

Whatever the case, her lack of concern about my involvement with Bill was fine with me. I felt we could continue indefinitely. Our relationship certainly hadn't harmed his political career, his marriage was still intact, and he and I were happy.

Seven

Bill Clinton is truly a sexual animal . . . in the best sense of the word. And sex with him was an absolute adventure. From that first heated embrace to our last tender good-bye, we could never seem to get enough of each other. During the twelve years of our relationship, our lovemaking, like the sex act itself, seemed to build from a strong, yet traditional start; through a fun and playful period; up to a mind-boggling, psyche-disturbing climax.

I knew the first night we made love that we were a perfect match sexually. He proved he could go on all night, and I was right there with him. Those early sessions, while dynamic and fulfilling, were somewhat traditional. As we grew more intimate, he wanted to expand, become more adventurous, which was fine by me. It was easy for us to get so turned on that we wanted to experiment and play games.

We would fantasize about what we wanted to do to each other and where we wanted to do it. When Bill passed by a furniture store with a bedroom set in the window, he would imagine having sex with me on that bed, in that window. Not likely to happen, I realize, but I think that fantasy was representative of how confined he felt in our relationship. We couldn't even do something so simple as go out for a drink together. So I think fantasizing about outrageous things made up somewhat for our inability to be together in public.

Bill and I made a pact early on: every day at noon, no matter where we were or what we were doing, we would stop and think of each other. Then he took it one step further: "When we think of each other, let's picture ourselves in bed, making wild, passionate love." It was our little secret. No one would ever know. I thought it was a sweet and exciting idea, and it reassured me that Bill cared enough about me to make a conscious effort to think of me in the middle of his busy days. Plus, I think it helped build even more passion into our relationship because it kept us turned on and anticipating getting together again.

Giving Bill gifts would have been a wonderful way to show him how much I cared about him. But it was out of the question. How could I give him something personal and not expect Hillary to notice? And how could he go into a store in Arkansas and buy a piece of jewelry, then not give it to his wife? So as much as I like getting gifts, I was happy just to get the occasional bottle of wine or single rose he sometimes brought to my apartment as a token of his affection. The truth is, making love with Bill was the greatest gift he could give me.

Occasionally, however, when he was out of town and away from curious eyes, he would buy me sexy lingerie. He said it was a turn-on just picking out the pieces and thinking about how they would look on me. I still have the things he gave me and will always treasure them. One is a tiny black teddy with thin straps and a lace inset that reveals just enough of my breasts to be provocative. As much as he loved for me to put that on for him, he was always more eager for it to come off.

He liked for me to model my sexy lingerie, dancing or moving around on the bed while he lay watching me. I loved seeing him get physically aroused. My sheer teddies revealed every curve underneath and really excited him. He would watch me for a few moments, then when he couldn't stand it any longer, he would gently take my hand, pull me to the floor, and slip the teddy off. The feel of his hands caressing my skin made me tremble with excitement, sending a surge of passion through him.

As we grew closer to each other, we naturally developed pet names for one another. I was his "Pookie" and he was "Baby" or "Darling" to me. Someone told me later that Pookie is a common pet name, but I had never heard it before, and thought it was cute. Even today, when I hear that name on TV or in a movie, it brings back warm memories.

Laughter was always a big part of our relationship, so we had fun creating pet names for our private parts as well. I called mine "Precious," and his penis was "Willard." "Why Willard?" I asked him "Because I always liked that name," he said. "You know, Willard for Willy!" And you know, it kind of had a Willard-like personality. Talking with each other so intimately and with gentle humor only added to our sexual pleasure.

When Bill would call me on the telephone, I knew immediately if other people were in the room with him, because the first thing he would ask was, "How are the girls?" I would laugh, knowing he was referring to my breasts. And I would respond in kind, "Fine.

How're the boys?" referring to his testicles. It was our way of saying something intensely private to each other in a very public setting.

The phone also played a part in our relationship when I was on the road or living away from Little Rock. Since we were unable to see each other regularly, he liked to call and entice me into phone sex. He would start by saying something provocative—Bill loved to talk dirty and to have me say sexy things back to him—and we would masturbate while we talked on the phone. To me it was fun to talk dirty to him because he got so excited, but most of the time I just pretended I was masturbating, because phone sex really didn't excite me. I prefer human contact . . . flesh to flesh. But Bill would keep it up until he climaxed while we were talking. It reached the point where every time he called, he'd want to have phone sex. I got uncomfortable with the whole thing, and I began making up excuses to put him off. Finally, I told him it just wasn't the same for me not to have him there in person, and that put an end to it.

While I was living in Little Rock we spent so much time in my apartment that we started to invent ways of entertaining ourselves. Obviously, sex took up much of our time together, but we both wanted to do other things, too. One night, Bill was watching me fix my makeup and he seemed interested in the whole process. I said "Let me put some of this on you." At first he demurred, but then agreed. I applied eye shadow, then some eyeliner and mascara. Before he could say no, I also put a little bit of blusher on his cheeks. He was astonished at how different he looked and asked me to do it again the next time we were together. He was absolutely fascinated by how different he looked with makeup on. I wonder if now, when the makeup people prepare him for TV appearances, he remembers the times we put makeup on him in my apartment.

Aside from some playful diversions like that, the main focus of our time together was sex, and it was on both our minds constantly. Bill wanted us to make love in his office in the Capitol building. He liked the idea of having sex on his desk or on the floor with all his staffers working right outside. I'm sure no one ever would have suspected anything was going on. Right. Especially Betsey Wright, his aide. I don't think her heart could have stood it. But I actually liked the idea, and one day, without warning, I made my way to his office with plans to fulfill his fantasy. Unfortunately, we met on the stairs as he was leaving for a meeting. He knew immediately why I'd come and the disappointment in his eyes was obvious.

We still had my apartment, though, and Bill continued coming up with different sexual experiments for us. One night he asked me to put on a short skirt with no underwear, then sit in a chair and cross and uncross my legs while he watched. He became so aroused just watching me, it was a thrill. He said he read about that move in a magazine, long before Sharon Stone wowed audiences with it in *Basic Instinct!* His fantasy was to have that scenario actually take place in a meeting someday.

Bill was happiest, however, with fantasies I could make happen for him. One night, I met him at the door wearing my fur coat with nothing on underneath but a white bustier, a garter belt with fur and lace on it, white stockings, and heels. He closed the door, and I slowly opened my coat for him. A look of astonished delight spread across his face. He drew a sharp breath, grabbed me, and tore at the garter belt as he carried me to the bedroom.

He made love to me that night as if he were possessed. It was enormously satisfying to know I could arouse and please him so easily. Kindling the sparks of passion in him became a challenge for me. I spent hours inventing ways to thrill him. My little white outfit had excited him so much, I decided to surprise him with it again—only under more dangerous circumstances.

One day he was attending a meeting, and asked me to meet him at the Excelsior Hotel. He had gotten a room and was waiting for me there. I strolled into the hotel wearing my fur coat with Bill's favorite white bustier and little else on underneath. When he opened the door to our room, he knew from the way I was holding my coat closed exactly what was in store for him. He closed his eyes for a second, fighting to control his passion. Then he eagerly pulled me into the room and slowly opened my coat to confirm his expectations. He groaned with pleasure and had me on the floor within seconds.

As time passed, Bill became even more inventive in his sexual games. He was always looking for ways to enhance our sexual pleasure and constantly came up with interesting ideas for us to try. So when he suggested dripping ice on my body, I was eager to try it. The first cold drop sent a little tremor through me. But he soon had me moaning with pleasure as he held the ice over my naked body, slowly letting the icy water drip onto my nipples and slide down to my stomach. As he continued, moving it back and forth, dripping it all over me, I got so excited I couldn't wait for him to make love to me. But he teasingly tortured me, making me wait until I couldn't stand it any longer, then entering me and slowly building the tension even further until we reached a climax beyond anything we'd ever experienced together.

He had a way of making me want to do anything he asked. After all, we both came of age during the sexual revolution of the '60s and '70s and each of us had enjoyed that new-found sexual freedom. For example, with Bill, oral sex seemed like the natural thing to do. I was a little surprised, though, when he came in my mouth the first time we did it. I wasn't expecting it and I guess the shock showed on my face, because he was suddenly very concerned, asking me what was wrong. I told him I wasn't prepared for that (sexual revolution or not) and how I hadn't planned for it to happen until I was married— or maybe never. He kind of smiled and held me close. I think he enjoyed knowing how much power he already had over me.

It seemed the more I agreed to do with Bill, the further he wanted to go with his games. Mostly that was okay with me, but I reached a point where I became a little afraid. I saw a movie in which a woman dripped candle wax all over some guy. Bill liked the idea and wanted me to do the same to him, but it sounded painful and I couldn't bring myself to do anything that might hurt him. I did, however, agree to spank him during sex play, and he got a big thrill out of it.

I laugh to myself when I hear reporters talk about Bill's love of food, because at one time in our experimenting, food became a sensuous toy for us. I had a little plastic honey jar shaped like a bear. Bill would slowly squeeze the honey all over my body, then sensually rub it all over me. It was very erotic. We also loved to sit on the floor and play sex games using all sorts of food. He would blindfold me, then go to the kitchen and look for things that would feel sensuous in my mouth. I loved it when he would slowly pour juice into my mouth until it overflowed, and little streams of liquid would trickle down my naked body. Before long we'd both be so turned on, he'd be rubbing this smooth, gooey mixture all over me. He'd take me to the bed, I'd pull him down on top of me, and we'd make love. What a sensation!

Being a controlling person myself, it was a huge expression of sexual trust for me to let him blindfold me. Although my hands were free, I felt extremely vulnerable because I didn't know what he might do. But that's what made it so exciting—not knowing what would happen next! It was exciting to him, too, because he was the one controlling the fantasy. Often we would switch roles and I would be the one controlling the fantasy.

After those food fests we'd both be covered with ketchup and milk and whatever, so we'd hop in the shower. Showering together was one of our favorite pastimes, but Bill especially liked to give me baths. I would sit in the tub, and he would get his hands all soapy and run them over my body. On one occasion I came out of the bath, brushing my hair, and Bill looked at me and said, "Let me do that." He gently drew the brush through my hair, talking to me softly. It became a regular routine after that. I thought it was sweet to have this big, macho guy doing such a gentle, personal thing.

One night he suggested tying me to the bed, but I balked at the idea. As much as I trusted him, I just couldn't bring myself to give him that much physical control over me. When I wouldn't let him tie me up, he asked if I would do it for him. Now that didn't bother me at all. In fact, I loved the idea.

I pulled some silk scarves from my dresser and tied his hands to the metal bedposts. He was completely at my mercy, and I took advantage of it. I teased him and played with him until he was almost out of his mind with excitement. It turned both of us on so much that we did it again several times. Bill, as always, wanted to take it a step further, so the next time I tied him to the bed, he asked me to use a dildo-shaped vibrator on him. It was exciting to see him getting so aroused, and I couldn't wait to untie him so he could use it on me.

Bill loved sexual adventure and he taught me to love it too. But our escapades finally reached a point where I became concerned. The sexual relationship became overwhelming and all-encompassing. All I could think about was our sex games: what we had done to each other the night before and what we might do the next day. I spent my days in a trance, pretending to work and function like a normal person, but all the while being obsessed with all that we were doing.

In looking back, I believe we were addicted to the sexual excitement. It was almost like being addicted to a drug. As the addiction increased, we craved more and more sex at a higher intensity. The whole experience is something that I've never gotten over psychologically. And, though I can't deny enjoying it—it was indescribably erotic—I never want to repeat it.

★ ★ ★ ★

During our twelve years together, Bill rarely asked me to do something that was totally repugnant to me. Except for one time. He tried to set up a threesome with another woman, but I told him in no uncertain terms that I was not interested. I know people say, "Never say never," but anything that goes beyond two people is too kinky for me and I thought he knew that.

At times, through the years, I had wondered just how far he would take his experimentation, but he'd never mentioned wanting to see me with another woman. And I had certainly never given him the idea it was something *I* wanted to do. Yes, we had discussed a threesome before, but never as something that would be a possibility for us. I guess I had just given him so much leeway already, he thought he'd give it a try. He apologized for suggesting it, and never did so again.

When the Troopergate scandal broke and allegations surfaced of Bill's having used prostitutes, I figured he fulfilled his fantasy of a threesome with them. I became concerned about my health in light of the charges that he had been with prostitutes. If the stories were true, what diseases might he have exposed me to? He never used a condom when we had sex, and I never asked him to. I thought the only thing I had to worry about was birth control. Since then, I've been tested for AIDS and, thankfully, have tested negative. But I was angry that he so casually exposed me to that kind of danger without my knowing it.

When I first saw the list of women named in Larry Nichols' lawsuit, there was only one woman I suspected might have had an affair with Bill—Deborah Mathis. From our days together as reporters at KARK-TV, I knew Deborah was an attractive, sexual person. Well, so was Bill. They would have spent lots of time together while Deborah was doing stories, just as Bill and I had. And early in our relationship he *had* warned me not to get too chummy with her.

He and I talked about that list of women when it was released. He went down the names and explained them all away. All except Deborah. He said, "I've talked to Elizabeth Ward maybe three times in my whole life." Elizabeth Ward was a former Miss America whom

Larry had linked to Bill. He went on to explain his connection with Lencola Sullivan, a former Miss Arkansas, whom Larry had also named. "At least Lencola Sullivan is a friend of mine even though I haven't ever slept with her," Bill told me. Susie Whitacre was his press secretary, and of her he said, "Poor little Susie's a good Catholic girl. She came to the mansion once or twice to do work with me. That's how her name made the list." But nothing about Deborah.

Today, Deborah Mathis has her own syndicated column with Tribune Media Services. She's frequently seen at White House press conferences, and Bill never fails to call on her. Coincidence? I seriously doubt it.

I could brush aside that group of women, but when Bill's former state troopers started spilling the beans about his escapades with dozens of other women, I thought long and hard about it. I have no way of knowing if this is true about the other women, but I think Bill felt an enormous sense of power from leading me into sexual adventures, so he very likely enjoyed using that power and influence he had as governor to conquer other women, too. Lots of women have the "groupie" mentality and make themselves available to men of power and fame. I think Bill was addicted to the chase, not the sex act itself, but the actual conquering of all those women. The challenge of finding the places and times he was able to pull it off added to the excitement. And it must have been enormously flattering to have women seek him out and want him sexually.

Back in his high school days, he was just a guy in the band. He wasn't a big, muscular football hero who had girls falling all over him. Then all of a sudden, he became a politician and started getting the kind of attention he had only dreamed of. My gut feeling is that, yes, there were a lot of other women, particularly when I was living away. But if he managed to play nasty with as many women as they say he did, he's even more of a man than I thought he was!

When I came back to Little Rock, we were seeing each other so frequently that if he was able to carry on with a number of women besides me, then the son of a bitch deserves a medal. I would have to question when he had time to be governor, because he would have had to be having sex all the time, practically day and night. He may have stepped up his activities after we broke up, because I really felt I left a gaping hole in his life. Maybe he set out to do whatever he could to try to fill that emptiness.

Bill knew I saw other men occasionally during our twelve years together; that was never a secret. But if I'd had the slightest suspicion he was seeing women to the degree people have claimed he was, I would have booted his butt out.

In 1994, when I learned that Paula Corbin Jones was suing Bill for sexual harassment, I was shocked. I find it difficult to believe that he sexually harassed her in the true definition of the term. I'm betting she willingly went to that hotel room. She's a girl from a little town who was excited about Bill showing her some interest. They may have played around a little bit, but I imagine it was consensual. I think after the troopers made her name public, she felt a need to cover herself and save her reputation.

Paula said right out that Bill told her he didn't want her to do anything she didn't want to do. That statement in itself makes the sexual harassment charge look pretty shaky. She is probably typical of girls like her who were raised around that area. They don't like to admit that they're too far beyond a virgin. Bill didn't need to force women to have sex with him. He had no trouble finding any number of willing participants.

I often wonder if Bill has continued his womanizing ways now that he's in the White House. My guess is he probably has. I don't imagine it's been easy for him, but a leopard doesn't change its spots that quickly. I've heard speculation that he and Barbra Streisand had a thing. She went so overboard while Bill was campaigning, gushing over him and buddying up to his mother. She seemed like a woman hypnotized, and Bill loves that kind of mindless adoration. But, boy, can I relate to feeling hypnotized. He certainly has that effect on women.

Every time I hear new reports about Bill and the women he's allegedly been with, it hurts. I still believe that what we had was not a 12-year affair, but rather a relationship. I really loved that man and still carry warm memories of him in my heart. Not a day goes by that I don't think about some of the good times we had, the loving times, and it's sad that so much pain has happened to both of us since then.

My dad, Gene Flowers, who died in 1973. His personality was just as captivating as his good looks.

I was always so bundled up in frigid Alaska that Mother called me her "Little Eskimo."

Look at all those freckles!

Even as an angelic-looking six year old I had dreams of fame, but I never anticipated notoriety!

In costume, ready to perform.

Posing with my mother, Mary, right after I recorded my first record, "There Ought to be a Law." I insisted on the sunglasses because now that I was a recording star, I was just sure someone would recognize me!

Showing off my new bicycle.

Mother and Daddy
together in the 1950s.

I won a trophy for this
performance in a talent show
when I was ten years old.

For a time, cheerleading was more important to me than singing. I'm the one in front, doing the splits.

I was president of the Young Arkansans for Rockefeller while Winthrop Rockefeller was running for governor. That's me, right smack in the middle, with my boyfriend, Joe Clifton, standing behind me.

In late-sixties' formal finery for a Sigma Alpha Epsilon fraternity formal with Joe.

My dad (on the right) and my Uncle Curt
Horne were known as "High" and "Pressure."
Daddy was "Pressure."

I couldn't wait to graduate and
move on to more exciting things.

Joe and I (on the left) cut
loose and went wild once
we reached the University
of Arkansas. This picture
was taken at another SAE
frat party—not quite as
formal this time!

"Easy Living" was one of the first
bands I organized and managed.

In the recording studio
during the early days
of my singing career.

As back-up singers for the Roy Clark Show, our threesome was called "Fanci."

Doing what I love
best—singing.

This is another of my bands. We sang together during the early seventies.

The Justice Building in Little Rock, where Bill Clinton made his first move on me—asking for my phone number. The Capitol Building is in the background.

This is the Governor's Mansion in Little Rock, where Bill and Hillary lived. I performed at a party there, and Bill tried to persuade me to sneak into the men's room and make love.

Bill bought this little black nightie for me. He liked me to model it for him, but it never stayed on long!

My apartment, #2J in the Quapaw Tower, with the balcony visible just above the tree in the center of the picture. I would stand on the balcony when I knew Bill was coming over and wait for him to jog into view.

When I would spot Bill jogging down the street, I'd race downstairs and prop this side door open with a newspaper so he could sneak in unnoticed.

This is the bed that Bill and I spent so many happy hours in. Bill loved to have me tie his hands to the metal posts.

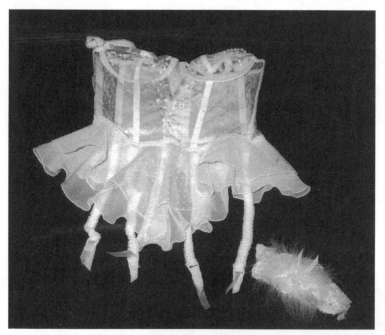

I liked to meet Bill at the door wearing nothing but this white bustier, garter and high heels. It was his favorite outfit!

This picture was taken in Bob Guccione's house in New York. I'm seated at a piano that belonged to Judy Garland. It's completely covered with gold leaf.

With actress Ruta Lee at the Thalian Ball in Hollywood.

Left to right: me, Jessica Hahn, and Rita Jenrette on the set of HBO's *Dream On*. Jessica grabbed a lot of attention with her see-through top.

Autographing copies of *He Said, She Said*. I signed over 700 magazines that day.

Morton Downey Jr. is as sweet as he can be. I appeared on his radio show—we really hit it off.

Enjoying a quiet dinner in Madrid, Spain, with my boyfriend, Finis Shelnutt. Finis has stood by me through thick and thin.

One of my many
appearances on radio talk
shows. I enjoy doing radio
shows. Talking with people
one on one helps dispel a
lot of the myths created
about me.

A rare relaxing moment
at my mom and dad's
home on the lake.

Underneath all that
makeup, Tammy Faye
Bakker is real cute.
But even with the
makeup she's a sweet
and genuine person.

My wonderful, supportive parents: Mary and Jim Hirst.

In Madrid, surrounded by the ever-so-polite and respectful Spanish press in the studio of the *De Tu a Tu Show*.

Actor Rip Taylor (left) has become a favorite of mine and Finis. We met him at the Thalian Ball in 1992.

For Bill's birthday in August 1994, I imitated Marilyn Monroe's tribute to John F. Kennedy and sang "Happy Birthday Mr. President." Comedy Central came up with the idea, and it was a lot of fun. (*Photo by Frank Micelotta*)

I met my dear friend
Marjorie Moore when we
were both working at the
Cipango Club. Margie has
been a rock of support
since the day we met.

Every once in a while, Finis and I
sneak away for a little R & R.

I treasure every moment I spend with my mother, like this one at the
Thalian Ball in 1994. Even though she didn't approve of my affair with
Bill, she has always been one of my greatest defenders.

Eight

THUNDER IN THE DISTANCE

The '80s were coming to an end, and though I didn't know it, so
was my amazing love affair with Bill Clinton. I had been singing
in various places around Little Rock, but had finally signed a contract
with the Excelsior Hotel. I was excited about this booking. The
Excelsior was the nicest hotel in town, full of wonderful memories
for me, since Bill and I had rendezvoused there many times. I was
looking forward to a long-term arrangement with the hotel. By then,
I had been back in Little Rock four years, and this was by far the most
lucrative engagement I had secured yet.

During this time, a friend approached me and suggested a blind
date with a buddy of his. I said I wasn't interested. I hated blind dates.
Besides, Bill and I were heavily involved again, and I couldn't have
cared less about meeting someone else.

The same friend also wanted to introduce me to a man who was
trying to get funding to build a music theater in Harrison, Arkansas,
a small town in the Ozarks just south of Branson, Missouri. I was
always interested in hearing about new business opportunities. Even
though I planned to be at the Excelsior a long time, it never hurt to
make new contacts that could pay off in the future. So I agreed to a
luncheon to hear about the new theater.

We all met at Fu-Lin's Chinese Restaurant on South Victory
Street in Little Rock, just a block away from the governor's office.
Halfway through my chow mein, I started asking the gentleman
questions about the plans for his music theater. His blank stare told
me he had no idea what I was talking about. I looked quizzically at
my friend and his guilty smile gave it away. I thought this was the
business lunch, but it was really the blind date.

I chuckled to myself and turned back to my "date," looking at
him from a different perspective. What I saw intrigued me. His name
was Finis Shelnutt, and he had the bluest eyes I'd ever seen—real cute!
His tweed jacket gave him a comfortable and casual air. And, although

he was recently divorced and seemed vulnerable, he also appeared to be solid and stable.

I asked about his unusual name. It seems he was the last-born in a family of four boys. His mother decided this would be her last child, and while she was pregnant she announced to her husband that she was *finis*. To emphasize her point, she put it in writing—on the birth certificate. We both had a good laugh over that and I found myself drawn to this man more than I had been drawn to anyone in years. (Although it wouldn't have meant anything to me at the time, I found out much later that Finis' former brother-in-law is Webster Hubbell, Bill's best friend and golfing buddy who went to Washington with him, but left in disgrace and is now facing prison. Webb was also one of Hillary's law partners.)

We finished lunch, and even though I had been duped, I didn't mind. I'd enjoyed meeting Finis and hoped I would see him again. As we left the restaurant, he showed me his pride and joy: a black Porsche 928S. I smiled to myself, "Boy, if he's trying to impress me he's doing a great job!"

I thought sure Finis would call right away and ask me out, but he didn't. In fact, I didn't hear a word from him for nearly two months. My friend who had introduced us called me one day to ask if Finis had been in touch with me. I told him no, and said I was surprised and a little disappointed. I thought we had hit it off the day we met and couldn't understand why he hadn't called. So our matchmaking friend got busy again.

It was Christmas time, and within a few days I finally heard from Finis. He called to invite me to our friend's Christmas party. He also asked me to go to his company Christmas party with him. He was a vice president with Southtrust Bank of Alabama and ran its investment office in Little Rock. Although I was happy he called, I was real busy preparing for my booking at the Excelsior Hotel and needed to rehearse every night. Finis was insistent, though. He told me he would start the party two hours earlier than he had planned and take me home whenever I needed to go. How could I resist such an accommodating offer?

The party was lovely, good food, good wine, and a good view of his cute little butt as he excused himself to go to the men's room. (Hmm . . . maybe there was a third date in this after all.) True to his word, he brought me home early so I could rehearse. He apologized for not contacting me sooner, and shocked me when he told me the reason he hadn't called before was he didn't think someone as beautiful as I was could be interested in him. The man had a way with words.

During the twelve years Bill and I had been together, I had met many interesting men, but not one of them had made my heart do flip-flops like Bill had done. Not until Finis. I was starting to like everything about him: the fact that he was successful in the fast-paced, chance-taking financial world; the way he willingly changed the party plans so I could be included; his gentlemanly manners whenever we were together; and of course, his cute little butt. This guy was something else.

We started seeing each other regularly. He would come to the Excelsior and stay until I finished singing, at midnight, even though he had to get up early for work. He was quite attentive and eager to spend lots of time with me. As we grew closer to each other, I had a strong feeling this relationship might work out.

Finis was so different from all the other men I had dated in my futile attempt to disconnect myself from Bill. I couldn't quite put my finger on what it was about him . . . until I put my fingers on "Big Tex." I knew there was something special about that man.

I had a big problem, though. I knew I couldn't give a relationship with Finis a fair shot as long as my mind was clouded with Bill Clinton. Bill still had a lot of influence on me, and I needed to get away from him so I could have a clear head for this relationship—to see if it had the potential I thought it did.

For the first time in my life, I started to seriously consider settling down. I was even open to giving up my singing career. It had never been easy to date men who worked during the day when I worked at night. Going out with men who worked daytime jobs usually consisted of their coming to the club where I was singing at night. Finis went through that, spending a lot of time at the Excelsior, and I know it was hard on him. I actually began thinking seriously about getting out of the entertainment business.

But first, I had to do something about Bill. Even though I knew what my decision would have to be, it was excruciatingly difficult. We had been together twelve years, and the affection we had for one another ran deep. I forced myself to look at our relationship realistically and honestly. Although we'd shared twelve wonderful years of romantic involvement, nothing was ever going to come of it. I had known that for years, but I loved him enough to not let it matter. Now there was a new man in my life, and I couldn't let my affection for Bill jeopardize the new and exciting relationship that was building with Finis. Hard as it was, I made my decision.

Bill came to see me one night, and we made love for what I was determined would be the last time. But once in his arms, I could feel my resolve melting. How could I give this up? This was the man I had been closer to than any other. We knew each other so well and had shared so many memories. Did I really want it to end? I took a deep breath, drew on every ounce of inner strength, and forced myself to do what I knew I had to. As he was leaving, we sat on the couch and I pulled him close and gently told him it would be our last time together. I told him I had met someone I cared for, someone I wanted to devote myself to. We both knew I couldn't do that as long as part of me still belonged to him.

He was quiet for a moment, then tears began to roll down his face. Like me, he couldn't believe the inevitable was at hand—our years of love and passion had finally come to an end. He choked back his tears as he told me, "I understand, and I want you to do what you need to do for your life." As strong as I was determined to be, I burst into tears, too. Bill Clinton had been the major focus of my life for so long, and severing the bond between us was one of the hardest things I've ever had to do.

I knew I had to do this. I had to make the break and move on, but his pain hurt me badly. If there was ever any doubt that I filled a tremendous void in his life, he erased it that night. As he left, he turned to me and said softly, "If you ever change your mind and you ever want me to come back, all you have to do is call me."

I felt terrible after he left—hurt by the break-up and worried about him. He may have had flings with other women besides me, but I knew in my heart I was special to this man, as he was to me. But I had grown and matured. I had now experienced enough to know I needed someone in my life on a regular basis. And that someone could not be a married man. Here I was, proceeding with my life with someone I cared about, looking forward to a wonderful life, and Bill was still stuck in an unhappy marriage, and he didn't have me to fill that void anymore.

He pleaded with me to keep in touch, saying, "Please, let's talk;

let's just talk by phone. Let me know what you're doing, what's going on." I was glad he said that. I couldn't imagine cutting off all communication with him—it would have been like slicing off an arm. So we did talk frequently. I was always happy to hear from him and was gratified that he seemed to be getting his life in order and moving forward with his political plans. More often than not, when we talked he would try to convince me that we should get back together, but I wasn't willing to do that. Finis and I were becoming increasingly close, and I didn't want to jeopardize that.

Several months after Bill and I broke up, Finis and I spent an afternoon at the horse races in Hot Springs, and I saw Bill for the first time since our final night together. Finis had gone to get us something to drink, and I was sitting alone in our box. I heard a buzz in the conversation around me, then heard someone say, "There's the governor." I turned around, and, sure enough, there was Bill, smiling in my direction. He came over and sat down next to me. As usual, people were staring, and he couldn't have cared less. I was relieved Finis wasn't there. I hadn't told him of my relationship with Bill and didn't think it was the most appropriate time to enlighten him. Bill and I had a short, but friendly conversation. As he left, he smiled, but with a wistful look in his eyes.

★   ★   ★   ★

Bill was in the last stages of his final campaign for governor in 1990 when a former employee, Larry Nichols, filed a lawsuit against him. Bill had fired Larry for purportedly making unauthorized long-distance telephone calls to the Contras, and Larry retaliated later by filing a lawsuit. The lawsuit charged Bill with using state funds to finance his romantic trysts with several unnamed women and five whom he specifically identified—including me. I knew nothing about the lawsuit until Finis called to tell me his investment firm had received a press release listing all five women. Investment firms receive all sorts of odd information. So Finis called and said rather ominously, "I need to talk to you about something."

When he brought the press release over and I read it, my heart sank. I told him, "Look, I don't want you to be worried about this. I'm sorry it's come into your office." Naturally, his office was all abuzz about it. I said again, "Let's just not worry about it," but the tears began rolling down my face. Finis and I had been dating for almost a year, and things had been going smoothly. I could just picture it all going to hell, and I was extremely upset. He was amazingly restrained and didn't ask me directly if it was true. He didn't push the issue. Instead, he was very comforting and I was grateful to him for that.

As soon as Finis left, I headed for the telephone to call Bill. But I stopped short and started thinking. My friends had been telling me for years that I should tape my telephone conversations with Bill just in case anything bad ever happened and I needed some proof of our relationship. I had always laughed them off; this was a man I had loved and cherished for years . . . I knew he would never hurt me. But what about his friends and colleagues? My devotion to Bill had blinded me to the reports and rumors that had begun to surface about what happened to those who tried to cross or became a threat to that all-powerful Arkansas power structure that stood behind Bill Clinton. Whenever these things came up in our discussions, he always had an excuse or an explanation. And I never wanted to push it. But, for the first time, I thought it might be wise to take my friends' advice.

I had a little tape recorder that I used when I did verbal contracts over the phone for singing engagements. Before I dialed Bill's number, I hooked it up to the telephone and turned it on. I wasn't entirely sure how it could help me, but I knew I didn't like what was developing. My name surfacing publicly all of a sudden made me nervous . . . especially since Bill and I weren't even seeing each other any longer!

When I reached Bill, he explained the whole thing away, reminding me he was in the midst of a gubernatorial race and pointing out that this lawsuit was just a ploy to discredit him. He felt sure it was a set-up by his opponent, Sheffield Nelson, to make him look bad and to cost him the election. He succeeded in calming me down, and promised he'd take care of things. Which is exactly what he did. He had the lawsuit moved into the court of a judge he had appointed, the judge sealed the case, denied the subpoenas, and it was eventually dismissed. Bill had been governor most of the years since 1978, and he was The Power; there weren't many strings he couldn't pull.

None of this seemed to have any effect on the election. Bill won, and things quieted down again. I naively thought everything would be okay. I even felt a little silly about taping the conversation and told myself I'd been watching too many movies.

★ ★ ★ ★

Although I didn't know it at the time, my life was beginning to change. I was still singing at the Excelsior, but my nights had been cut back. The economy was starting its slide into recession, and the entertainment business was suffering. Most places were cutting corners, using bands on a part-time basis or maybe just a piano player. For the first time in my career, I was having difficulty making enough money singing to support myself.

During this time, I received some devastating news: Mother had cancer. She had found a lump in her breast and the doctor wanted to do a biopsy. My stepfather called me at 9:30 the morning of the biopsy and said, "It is cancer and they're going to do the mastectomy tomorrow morning." I lined up someone to substitute at the club for me and got in the car and drove up there.

I remember how long the drive seemed that day. It was hot and raining, and the roads were slick. I was so upset, screaming at the top of my lungs asking God, "Why are you doing this to us?" I felt so angry. My daddy had been taken from me when he was only 49; my mom was not even 60 yet. I thought, "Why don't you just give the cancer to me, God?"

At 3:30 that afternoon, I walked into her hospital room and said, "Well, we're going to have to just kick the devil right in the ass on this one." She agreed with me that she needed to be strong, but that was when she was still feeling strong psychologically and physically, before the surgery and all those horrible chemotherapy and radiation treatments.

I knew it was also important that I be strong. When she opened her eyes and looked into my face, I wanted her to see that strength. My stepfather and I took turns staying with her so that one of us was always in the room if she needed something or wanted a hand to hold.

Part of being strong was trying to maintain a sense of humor, because my mom always had a great one. She had the mastectomy on her birthday and I remember saying to her later, "Well, Mom, you sure know how to have a birthday." She laughed and said, "Boy, isn't that the truth?"

We looked for things to laugh about, but it wasn't easy. All I wanted to do was cry. I couldn't eat and I didn't sleep well. I quit wearing mascara during that time because I was afraid if I broke down and cried when I was out of the room, she would see the black smudges under my eyes and know.

It was a traumatic time for all of us. She went through a year-long series of chemotherapy and radiation treatments, and she needed a lot of emotional support to get through the ordeal. We'd talk on the phone, and I'd tell her to stay strong, to not get weak-minded. Then I'd hang up the phone and cry my eyes out. If I could have taken that cancer from her body and put it in mine, I would have gladly endured all of that pain for her. I would have done it in a second.

People have asked me if what I've gone through over my relationship with Bill Clinton and its repercussions is the worst thing that's ever happened to me. And, although it's been horrible and I've felt lonely and betrayed, it's never been anywhere near as bad as what I went through when Mother had that cancer. I'm so grateful that today she is cancer-free and enjoying every bit of her life.

During the time of her recovery and treatments, I was trying to spend as much time as I could with her, but I was getting a little desperate. Little Rock was close enough that I could drive to be with her in just a few hours, but I wasn't making enough money there. If I moved back to Dallas or someplace else where I had a better chance of full-time work, I would be so far away from her that I couldn't see her as often as I needed to. Plus, there was Finis to think about. Even though we had weathered the crisis over Larry Nichols' press release, our relationship wasn't as rock-solid as it had been earlier. The foundation of trust I had built with him was showing a few cracks. I knew if I left town, our romance would fall apart completely.

I had to find a way to stay in Little Rock. So I called Bill and asked if he could help me get a state job. I figured if I had a steady job I could stay in Little Rock, be near Mother, and sing whenever I could to supplement my income. He said he would get to work on it right away. "I'll call Judy Gaddy," he said. Judy's husband, Bill Gaddy, was the head of the employment security division for state government, and Judy was a governor's aide. Bill told me, "I'll have Judy call you and we'll find something for you."

Judy arranged an interview for me with a government agency that would have me traveling to nearby states to promote Arkansas through presentations to schools and organizations. However, someone with some clout had another person in mind, and Judy didn't make it evident enough to them that *I* was to get the job. They didn't hire me. I called Bill and asked, "What happened? I didn't get the job." Exasperated, he said, "I didn't stay on top of it like I should have. Don't worry. It won't happen next time."

My next interview was with the Arkansas Appeal Tribunal. The appointed head of the Board of Review, which encompassed the Appeal Tribunal, was Don Barnes, who had been appointed by Bill. Bill called Don and asked him to find something for me. Don was eager to accommodate him and came up with a strategy. He promoted a supervisor to be his personal assistant. Then he upgraded her former position so that it paid more, and opened it up for me.

To make sure everything looked on the up-and-up, I went through certain procedures. First, Don had to interview in-house to see if there were any qualified applicants. Charlette Perry, an eminently qualified black woman who had been with the Tribunal five or six years, interviewed for the job, but didn't get it. By claiming not to have found anyone qualified for the job within, Don could open up the position to the public and advertise in the newspaper. That's when I came in. Numerous people applied for the job, and the staff narrowed the list down to ten—of which I was one.

Randy Wright was the head of the Appeal Tribunal, and he conducted the interviews. My interview went smoothly—Randy and I hit it off immediately. Don Barnes sat in on my interview, and afterward suggested Randy hire me. Randy was easily influenced and eager to please his boss, and besides, he had liked me, too. So it was a done deal. I got the job, and it didn't bother me a bit that the way I got it was a little unorthodox. This was the way things got done in Bill Clinton's Arkansas. I knew I could handle the job and would do well, and I was grateful for the steady income.

Charlette Perry, however, was not pleased. She still felt strongly that she should have gotten the job instead of me, so she filed a grievance, and a hearing was scheduled. I was really surprised. The way I got my job was *not* out of the ordinary, I thought, and I couldn't believe I was going to be questioned about it. Both Don Barnes and

Randy Wright were happy with me, and I thought everything had been arranged so nothing would look funny.

The grievance hearing committee consisted of approximately ten people, and the hearing itself was conducted like a courtroom trial. I had to wait out in the hallway of this musty old state building where there was nowhere to sit, so I perched on the edge of a table. There were other people gathered around and we made small talk . . . all the time I was wondering what they had to do with this hearing. I had never seen any of them before. The longer I waited, the more nervous I became. I was still pretty confident that Bill would make everything okay, but I was getting a little anxious about what types of questions they would ask me.

Finally, we were called into the hearing room itself, which was just slightly more inviting than the hallway. The people who were conducting the hearing were seated in a line at a table at the head of the room, looking like a group of turkeys peering over a log. Some of them were attorneys and some were not. Randy Wright and Don Barnes were there also.

As soon as the questions began, I became intimidated. This was not the line of questioning I had expected. They were asking me very pointed questions about how I heard about the job, and they asked them over and over—almost like an interrogation. I could tell they were trying to trip me up on details, and I had the very clear impression they suspected Bill was involved in getting me the position.

I was scared. I didn't want to lie, but I knew if I told the truth—that Bill Clinton had indeed arranged the job for me—all hell would break loose. I tried to appear calm and simply puzzled, but in control. I clasped my hands in my lap to keep them from shaking. I calmly and innocently told the grievance committee I had learned about the job from the newspaper. I stuck to that version of events and tried hard not to give any conflicting answers. I didn't want Charlette to have grounds for a lawsuit. Bill would certainly experience a backlash from his political enemies if the truth came out, and I couldn't even imagine what might happen to me. Thank goodness Don Barnes finally put an end to the questioning and the hearing broke up.

Charlette won the ruling, and the committee demanded she be given my position or that an equal position be created for her. I called Bill in a panic over the outcome and the possibility of losing my job, but he reassured me. "Don't worry about it," he said. "Barnes has veto power. He'll take care of it." Sure enough, Don vetoed the grievance committee's ruling, and it was over. I couldn't believe it! I was relieved but amazed. Why have a grievance procedure if one person can over-rule the decision for no good reason?

The only thing Charlette could have done at that point was file suit for discrimination. But she evidently didn't have the legal or financial support to do that so she just let it go. I knew she had gotten a raw deal, but she only suspected it—she didn't know for certain. She was a hard worker, and I let her take charge of her area; she did a hell of a job of it. I admired her in a lot of ways: she had no husband and was the sole supporter of her three kids. Because she wasn't absolutely sure she had been sidestepped in favor of me, we had no problem working together.

I have no idea where Charlette Perry is today. She seems to have dropped completely out of the picture. I've often wondered if, after the story broke about Bill's and my relationship, she wasn't threatened to ensure she kept her mouth shut.

Once the hearing was over, I thought everything would be fine. Finis and I were still seeing each other, my job was going well, and I had also gotten a part-time job singing a few nights a week at the Flaming Arrow Club, a private club located in the Quapaw Tower building I had moved from after Bill and I broke up.

Bill had been elected governor again and things had settled down. No more was being said about the Larry Nichols lawsuit. But it wasn't long until the national media started hearing rumblings that Bill might be considering a run for the presidency. So, now and then, reporters from outside Arkansas would come to town looking for anything they could dig up about him. Once they hit town, the first thing they would unearth was that lawsuit and the press release, and they would try to track down the women Larry Nichols had named. Not too much came of their efforts, though. The women they were able to find simply wouldn't comment. Eventually, however, a *Washington Post* reporter actually came by my office looking for me. Luckily, I was out of the office at the time. I was getting concerned, feeling like this might all be building up to something.

I knew Bill was going to run for president. He had never deviated from that desire the entire time we were together. He made a false start of sorts in 1988, but it didn't work out. But now he felt he was ready. Even before he made the official announcement, he told me he had made up his mind: this year, 1991, was the year. I was thrilled for him. Even though personally I felt he should have waited a little longer, I was proud to see him going after his dream. Little did I know that his dream was about to become my nightmare.

Nine

On October 3, 1991, standing on the steps of the Old Statehouse in Little Rock, Bill Clinton announced to hundreds of enthusiastic supporters that he was officially a candidate for president of the United States. I was thrilled for him.

The announcement was hardly out of his mouth, however, before the national media descended on Little Rock in force, like a bunch of piranha, rummaging around for anything they could find on Bill. Naturally, one of the first things reporters uncovered was the lawsuit Larry Nichols had filed. Even though Bill's judge friend had sealed the case, the filing was in the public record, and that lawsuit was exactly the kind of information reporters look for when they're digging for dirt.

I was still working at the Appeal Tribunal during the day and singing at the Flaming Arrow at night. Although Bill and I had quit seeing each other two years earlier, I realized what an explosive revelation it would be if the public learned that a presidential candidate had had a mistress for twelve years. Reporters started sniffing around almost immediately, trying to get information on me. I was getting strange calls at work, and unfamiliar faces started popping up both at the Appeal Tribunal and at the Flaming Arrow. I began to feel frightened about what might lie ahead.

Then, Ron Fuller, a Republican legislator in Arkansas who was very close to the Bush campaign, called me. I had met him a few years earlier while singing at the Capitol Club. He made me an offer: "I have some friends in the Republican Party who would be willing to give you fifty thousand dollars and a job in California if you'll just admit it's true you had an affair with Bill Clinton. You don't have to give any details, just say it's true."

I was scared! It was becoming obvious that certain people wanted very badly to reveal our affair to the public. But I had no intention of becoming a political pawn, nor of revealing something I considered no one's business but Bill's and mine. I told him I didn't want any part of his plan, I didn't want to talk about it, and not to bring it up again. Ron Fuller has since denied making that offer, of course, but I did tell Bill about it right after it happened. He was angry at first, but his anger quickly subsided when he saw an opportunity. He asked me to sign an affidavit that the Republican Party had made me an offer so he could stick them with it if anything else came out. He thought he could use it to discredit anything the Republicans said about him.

What to do? I wanted to help Bill out, but I didn't want to sign any legal documents. I decided just to let him think, for the time being, that I might be willing to sign. Fortunately, Bill didn't push me on it, and eventually the idea faded away.

I was away from the office for a couple of hours one day at a doctor's appointment. When I returned, the receptionist told me a reporter from the *Washington Post* had been by, asking for me. I cringed inside. I knew it was only a matter of time before I ran headlong into reporters. I hoped I would be convincing enough to persuade them there was nothing to the stories about Bill and me, but I really hated the idea of having to deal with them at all.

Then two or three different times, reporters called the Flaming Arrow looking for me. The manager of the club, John Cain, told me the *Dallas Morning News* had called and so had reporters from *Inside Edition*. Again, I had managed to miss them, but I had a feeling my luck wasn't going to hold out much longer.

I was right. As I arrived at the Flaming Arrow one evening a few days later, a reporter and a cameraman from *A Current Affair* ambushed me in the parking lot—firing questions, and waving microphones in my face. I brushed past them and hurried into the club, but they weren't about to give up so easily. Within minutes, one of them tried to get into the club, camera and all. John, visibly upset, kicked him out.

I frantically explained to John I had nothing to do with all the rumors flying around, and they just weren't true. That was my story and I had to stick to it. He tried to be understanding, but he said, "Gennifer, I don't want any problems. We don't need cameras in a nightclub." It was a private club, and oftentimes people came in with someone they weren't supposed to be with. The last thing John wanted was for his customers to get nervous and uncomfortable. I told John I was sure all the fuss would die down soon. But he was skeptical. I was booked to continue singing there through the end of the year, but he wasn't willing to take any chances. He asked me not to come back.

This was a big blow. My singing job provided me with a much-needed second income, and I was going to have trouble making ends meet without it. I was feeling dejected and frustrated and wondering when all this attention would end. I still hadn't leveled with Finis about my years with Bill, but I didn't think I'd be able to keep it from him much longer: Not a pleasant prospect, as I had already told him in so many words that the rumors about Bill and me weren't true. My life seemed to be crashing down around me, and I was running out of ideas to prop it back up.

Then Mother called. Someone had called her and without identifying himself said sarcastically, "You should be real proud of your daughter. She'd be better off dead." Mother was scared for me and wanted to know just what the hell was going on. I felt like I'd been punched in the stomach. Her name wasn't even Flowers then; it hadn't been since she married Jim. And they lived in a very small town in Missouri. Someone had gone to a lot of trouble to track her down. I panicked that they might try to harm my parents.

I took that phone call as a personal message: "We can get to your mother, girl." Whoever made that call hit me in my most vulnerable spot. As much as I hated all this, I could deal with threats as long as they were directed toward me. But the possibility that my actions might have dangerous consequences for my mother scared me to death.

I was learning more about the harm that often came to people who crossed Bill Clinton or the power structure that surrounded and supported him. It had been reported that the state troopers who worked for Bill often threatened and roughed up Bill's enemies. For example, an attorney named Gary Johnson lived next door to me in the Quapaw Tower. I didn't really know him other than to say hello when we met in the hall. But I had heard that he'd had a disagreement with the homeowners association of the building because he had installed a video camera overlooking the parking lot, and they told him he couldn't do that. They explained that he didn't own the exterior of the building, but he did own his portion of the interior. In response, Gary moved the camera from its perch overlooking the parking lot and placed it instead so that it had a view directly out his front door and down the hall. Because our doors were close together, he also got a very clear view of my apartment door. When rumors began circulating that Bill and I were having an affair, Gary let it be known that he actually had a videotape of Bill coming to my apartment. Big mistake. Not long after that, some large men forced their way into his place, beat him senseless and left him for dead. According to Gary, they kept asking where "the tape" was. Sure enough, the videotape with Bill on it disappeared.

Gary, it seems, was a double threat because he was also acting as counsel for Larry Nichols, the man who filed the lawsuit against Bill Clinton.

In another incident, a man named Wayne Dumon allegedly raped Bill's cousin. She had identified two other men but they both had alibis, so she claimed it was Dumon. There was never proof of vaginal rape—the semen was found outside her body on her clothes—and he denied doing it. But, while he was out on bail, the sheriff and this girl's father attacked him and cut off his testicles and left him for dead. His sons found him and got him to a hospital; the sheriff put the severed testicles on display in his office. Dumon sued the men and won, but was never paid any money. He was also sent to prison for rape, and an expert witness was not allowed to testify that it was not his semen found on the girl. As far as I know, he's still sitting in jail in Arkansas.

This is all public record, too, not just some story made up to discredit Bill Clinton. So with stories like those in mind, when my mother called about her threatening phone call, I became doubly frightened. I drove to Missouri almost immediately because I felt like I needed to reassure her that I was okay, even though I wasn't. After a few days spent trying to sort out all that had happened in the past week, I came home not feeling much better. But at least I convinced her I was holding up all right.

As soon as I got home from Missouri, I checked my answering machine for messages. Bill had called several times while I was gone and had left a message for me to call him that evening at the governor's mansion. His voice on the machine sounded a little preoccupied, which didn't make me feel any better. I wondered if he had even more bad news for me. The little tape recorder I had used to tape our conversation a year earlier was still hooked up to my phone, and I switched it on without hesitation and without feeling any of the foolishness I had felt the first time. My increasing paranoia was stronger than my fear of feeling foolish.

I called Bill at the mansion and was put right through. I couldn't wait to talk to him; I was depending on him to figure out how to stop this invasion into my life. Without too many preliminaries, I told him about losing my singing job because of the reporters hounding me and also about Mother's mysterious phone call. Bill was concerned. When I related how my response to the reporters had been stony silence, he said, "Good for you." He chalked it all up to Republican harassment, trying to get to him through me.

Bill assured me that as long as I maintained my silence, nothing would come of the reporters' attempts to link us. As long as we stuck together, he said, we'd be fine. I was concerned about my job at the Appeal Tribunal—after all, it was a state job and Bill had arranged for me to get it. I don't know if the way I got the job was illegal, but it was certainly unethical. I asked Bill what I should do if anyone asked me if he had been involved in my hiring. Again, he told me to just deny it. Even though that would be a total deception, at that point I was willing to do or say just about anything to make this nightmare go away.

Bill offered to use his influence to persuade John Cain to take me back at the Flaming Arrow. He was still thinking he could engineer anything he wanted without repercussions, but I was astonished he would risk establishing yet another link between us. I told him, "No, I think it's probably wise that I'm not in a place where reporters know they can find me." Still, he said once things died down a little, he'd use his influence to help get my job back. We ended our conversation, and I wasn't terribly reassured. Bill was still behaving as if he were bulletproof, but somehow I didn't think reporters from out of state would back off the way the local boys did.

During this time, every day seemed to bring new worries. I wasn't used to having my life spin out of control, and I vacillated between fear, frustration, and anger. As much as I would have liked to take matters into my own hands, I couldn't think of a thing to do that might help. I had to count on Bill to deflect attention from me, and I wasn't all that certain he could do so. As bad as things were, I couldn't imagine they would get worse. But they did . . . and quickly.

A week or so after I spoke with Bill, I came home to my apartments at the Forest Place Apartments (where I had moved after Bill and I broke up) and found the dead bolt on my door locked. Since I wasn't in the habit of locking the dead bolt, I thought maybe maintenance had been in to fix something and had locked the dead bolt when they left. But when I went inside, nothing had been done. That was curious. If maintenance had been inside to make repairs, they would *always* leave a receipt on the counter to show they had been there—for their own protection. But I looked around and there was nothing—no receipt and no signs they had worked on anything. I called the manager and asked if someone had been in, and she checked her records and told me that none of their people had been inside. It was a mystery.

The same thing happened a few days later, and again, no receipt. This time, however, I noticed that my telephone had been moved from the nightstand by the bed to the dresser a few feet away. And there was what looked like dirt from a shoe or something on the floor, at the corner of the dresser, that hadn't been there that morning. I called the manager and insisted that her maintenance crew must have been inside my apartment. "Someone's been in here with a key, 'cause they locked the dead bolt," I told her. But, once again, she checked her records, and said, "No, no one has been in."

In spite of all the recent happenings, it didn't click in my mind that it could be anyone other than building maintenance. I figured maybe one of the crew knew I was gone all day, so he sneaked in to make phone calls or just hide out for awhile. I was exasperated— it was just one more irritation stacked on top of an already-large pile. Boy! Was I naive. I wrote a formal letter of complaint to management and insisted they follow proper procedure if their maintenance people needed to enter my apartment. Something screwy was going on and I wanted it on record that I had complained, just in case something turned up missing or I found some other problem.

A few days later, I came home to find the door ajar. Puzzled, I pushed it open, and stepped in. I couldn't believe my eyes; my whole apartment had been ransacked—furniture turned upside down, drawers emptied onto the floor, linens stripped off the bed. I was stunned. I dropped to my knees in the doorway and started shaking uncontrollably. This wasn't maintenance that had been inside my apartment. This was something much bigger, and I knew it had to be related to Bill. It scared me out of my mind.

For some reason, I didn't even think that someone might still be in my apartment. I just saw all the devastation and finally figured out just what was happening. I was so frightened and didn't want to be alone, so I called a friend and kept her on the phone while I started going through my things to see if anything was missing. I still shudder to think what might have happened if someone had been waiting for me!

I eventually let my friend go, and I put in a call to Bill. He wasn't at the mansion, but I hoped he would get back to me quickly to advise. I didn't bother calling the police . . . I knew this was a crime that would never be solved. It was a sickening process, going through the chaos they had left. It horrified and angered me to think that someone had touched and inspected nearly everything I owned. What a feeling of violation!

As I sifted through the mess, a chilling thought hit me: the person responsible for this might *not* be looking for something on Bill and me. This could be Bill himself, looking for what *I* had on *him*. But I couldn't imagine him thinking I was a threat. After all, I had tried to cooperate in every way I could to keep our affair quiet. Yet, looking around at what had been done to my apartment, I felt anything was possible. It was hard maintaining rational thought while standing in the midst of such destruction.

Thank goodness I had put the tapes of our conversations in what I thought was a safe place, away from my apartment, a few days earlier. Intuition told me I should do that, just in case. As far as I knew, the tapes were the only hard evidence of our relationship. But I had jewelry in my apartment . . . I had appliances, TVs, stereo equipment, all the normal things a burglar would be looking for. Nothing was missing. But it was obvious, everything in the apartment had been meticulously scrutinized.

My apartment had a long walk-in closet crammed full. Every item of clothing had been ripped off its hanger and thrown on the floor; everything on the shelves had been pulled down, gone through, and tossed on the floor; every shoe had been inspected to see if anything was inside. The intruders had even flipped my mattress over to check underneath. Boxes of photographs were scattered across the floor. I frantically searched my memory, trying to remember if a picture of Bill and me together had ever been taken. I didn't think so, but right then I wasn't sure of anything. It was like a scene from a bad movie. Although I was no expert, it appeared to have been done by professionals. Whoever ransacked my apartment knew what they were doing.

Standing amid the chaos, my emotions overwhelmed me. I felt

anger about what had been done to my apartment; frustration because the media attention had cost me my singing job; and panic because I knew the lid was close to blowing off the badly kept secret of my relationship with Bill. This was not a game—it was deadly serious. I didn't know whom I could trust—including Bill. I knew then that my life was in danger.

Bill called me back a short time later and, once again, I taped the conversation. No hesitation at all. I would add this tape to my growing collection, safely tucked away. He was upset about the break-in and asked me specifically if any of my phone records were missing. I kept detailed phone records for tax purposes because I conducted a lot of business on my personal phone. But local calls didn't show up on my bills, and the calls I made to him when he was out of town were usually to hotels. My phone records didn't present a problem as far as I could see. I thought Bill should be much more worried about the phone records at the mansion—all incoming and outgoing calls were logged, and I called him there frequently. Nor had he ever been reluctant to call *me* from the mansion.

Bill seemed different that night on the telephone. For the first time, he was distant with me. Obviously, he was concerned about what was going on and wanted to know the details, but I didn't sense a great concern for me personally. It was clear he was just gathering as much information as he could to mount a defense if it became necessary. There was no playful banter between us as there always had been—he was much more formal and guarded with me.

Our conversation left me uneasy, and I told myself, "Gennifer, you're on your own, kid." It was obvious he was now looking out for himself, and I had to do the same. I looked around my apartment, which was still turned upside down, and felt extremely vulnerable and unprotected. There wasn't much I could do that night to increase my security, and I wasn't convinced the creeps wouldn't come back, since they'd found nothing the first time. The very next day, however, just to make myself feel better, I installed a chain lock on my door that could be locked and unlocked from the outside. I gave the key to no one. If someone got in while I was gone during the day, they would have to physically break in. And if someone tried to come in while I was at home, I figured I would at least have a few seconds warning as they were breaking through the chain.

I thought it unlikely Bill would do anything to harm me. What frightened me was not knowing how far his supporters might go. This was Arkansas, where politics is a blood sport, and funny things happened to people all the time. If Bill's backers perceived me as the enemy, there was no telling what they might do to try to eliminate any threat I might pose. Bill was supported by some powerful and wealthy people in Arkansas who were very eager to see him become president.

For the first time, I began to see the value of the tapes I'd made of our telephone conversations, and I was glad I had them. If anything happened to me, the tapes could at least establish a link between Bill and me. If I were to have a mysterious accident, I knew my mother could take that proof and, hopefully, Bill, his people, or whoever, would be held accountable.

Before the dust had settled from the break-in, a deejay on a local talk show got hold of the press release that had been spread around right after Larry Nichols filed his lawsuit—the same release Finis had received in his office—and he read it on the air. Bill heard about it and called me, incensed. He told me to get a lawyer and have him write a threatening letter. This really concerned him, because, as Bill put it, that deejay "was a real big mouth."

Looking back, that poor guy was probably one of the only people in Little Rock with guts. Very few local people dared cross Bill Clinton. Even the local newspaper hadn't gone anywhere with the information in Nichols' lawsuit. A tiny article that didn't include any of the names of Bill's alleged girlfriends was as far as the newspaper went with it. Plus, a local columnist claimed to have gotten a denial from every woman named in the suit, but he never even tried to contact me. I thought at the time, however, that this deejay was one more nuisance among many, so I took Bill's advice and went to a lawyer. I had him write a letter threatening to sue the radio station if the deejay didn't stop the accusations, and he stopped.

Every time I managed to put out one fire, a bigger one flared up. I took Bill at his word when he said all I had to do was deny, deny, deny—no one could prove anything. So far it seemed to be working. I *wanted* to protect Bill. Even though our relationship was a thing of the past, I was still very fond of him. We had a lot of years between us that were enormously meaningful to me.

Bill feared, rightfully so, that if word of our affair leaked out, it would torpedo his candidacy, just as Gary Hart's bid for the presidency sank when his affair with Donna Rice became public. The last thing I wanted was for my involvement with Bill to harm his chances for the presidency. Also, any more publicity about this could be disastrous for my own career . . . and my life. I was just barely hanging on to my job at the Appeal Tribunal, and I really wanted to sing again. I knew there was no way I could land another singing job in Little Rock if reporters were constantly trailing and harassing me. Most important of all, there was Finis. I loved him, and we had talked seriously about marriage before all the rumblings of scandal started. Further publicity would damage our relationship, probably beyond repair. All I wanted was to reclaim my life, and I felt if I followed Bill's plan of complete denial, eventually interest would have to die down. Who could prove anything?

I soon found out. Reporters from the *Star* magazine hit town determined to ferret out a story. They dug around a little bit, but couldn't find me or any information of value. Then they got a lucky break that really helped them out. They were in a bar one night and struck up a conversation with three girls. They asked the girls, "By chance, do you know Gennifer Flowers?" Unfortunately for me, I had interviewed one of the girls a week earlier for a job at the Appeal Tribunal. During the interview, we determined we had a friend in common. She spilled this to the *Star* reporters, along with the exact information of where I was working. They offered her two hundred dollars if she could get my unlisted home phone number, which she immediately set about doing. With the glint of easy money in her eye, she called our mutual friend and told him I had asked her to call me at home, but she had lost my number. She got the number, and bam! The *Star* had all they needed, and they set out to nail me.

Sure enough, the *Star* reporters started calling, both at work and at home. I had an answering machine at home, so I could just ignore those calls, but at work I couldn't avoid them. Two or three times reporters tried to get me to talk, but I cut them short with the denial routine—I said there was nothing to any of the rumors—and refused to say any more. I had no interest in talking with these people.

Each morning during this time, I woke up feeling sick to my stomach with anxiety and wondering what new surprise awaited me that day. Another reason for my anxiety was that I knew it was time to tell Finis the truth. I asked him to meet me for dinner, and before

I said anything about Bill, I fortified myself with a few drinks. I took a deep breath and told him the whole story. With a shaky voice I told him about my relationship with Bill. I told Finis *he* was the reason I ended the affair, because I had fallen in love with him, and that he was the only man who was able to tear me away from Bill.

He sat there quietly, his face an unreadable mask. I continued, describing how reporters had been following me, trying to get me to talk, and how I was becoming increasingly nervous about the whole situation. When I reached the end of the story, I looked at Finis. So far he hadn't said a word, and I still couldn't tell from his expression what he was thinking. He sighed, and finally spoke. His first words expressed concern for me. He didn't seem surprised at all; I think he probably knew from the moment he read Larry Nichols' press release that it was true. But he was grateful I had finally come clean with him and was anxious about how I was handling all the pressure. He took it well, but I could sense he was sad. The distance between us had been growing ever since the press release fell into his hands, and I knew the gap would only get wider now. I felt so desolate that I started crying. But I knew there was nothing I could do to stop him from drifting away.

Everything and everyone I cared about was being affected. Each day seemed to bring a new loss. The power I had always had to control my own destiny was slipping away rapidly. Would I lose my life next?

Meanwhile, the *Star* was getting closer. One afternoon I had pulled my car up in front of my office to load some things. When I came out a few minutes later, with my arms full, I noticed another car had pulled in front of mine. I glanced at the car and saw a man in the back seat pointing what looked like a camera at me.

Startled, I guessed this might be the people from the *Star* who'd been trying to reach me. My first reaction was to make a scene or, at the very least, give them the finger. Fortunately, my rational mind took over, and I decided to pretend I hadn't seen them, get in the car, and get the hell out of there.

When I got home, I had a message on my answering machine from the *Star.* "I think you should know we are going to print an article about what we know of your relationship with Bill Clinton, and we would like to talk to you about it. We also have photographs of you." The message went on to say that if I had any doubts about what was going on, to call Dick Kaplan, who was the managing editor of the *Star.*

I was speechless. A million things went through my mind. They couldn't really do that, could they? Who did they think they were fooling with? I'd file a lawsuit so fast they wouldn't know what hit them. Could Bill do anything? What was I going to tell Finis? I was frantic. There had to be something I could do to stop this from happening.

I called Blake Hendrix, an attorney I had met while singing at the Excelsior. Blake and his girlfriend came into the lounge occasionally, and I had gotten to know them. He had handled some business for me in the past, and I hoped I could trust him. He reminds me a little of Miles Silverberg, the character on "Murphy Brown," only without Miles' neurotic temperament. Blake has that same boyish look and is extremely affable and approachable. I had been impressed with his intelligence and competence, and I desperately needed someone sharp to help me out.

He agreed to meet with me right away to talk about my problem, so I rushed over to his office. I filled him in on everything, from the very beginning with nothing left out, and told him my only desire was to stop this story—no matter what it would take. Blake listened carefully and seemed a little nervous. He said he would call Dick Kaplan, and on my order, threaten to sue. I was praying to God he could handle this for me. Any hopes I had were short-lived, however. I underestimated the power and drive of the media.

The *Star* wasn't compliant like the radio station had been. After Blake called Dick Kaplan to discuss the situation, he called me back and said, "Gennifer, I think we should get on a plane, go up there, sit down with these people, and try to reason with them." So on the basis of his advice, I convinced myself we could outmaneuver the *Star*, and I agreed to fly to New York. I called Bill before we left to tell him where I was going and what was going on with the *Star*. I panicked when he wasn't there, and was upset that he hadn't called me back by the time we left. I kept thinking, "Dammit, please hurry and call me back. I need you!" I had no way of knowing at that time that I would never speak to him again.

By this time, I was beginning to think that where Finis was concerned, it might be safer for him if I put some distance between us. So I didn't phone him before I left.

On the plane, with Blake seated beside me, I thought about the upcoming confrontation and naively believed I had the upper hand.

I was certain once Dick Kaplan saw me in person and saw how adamant and willing to sue I was, he would back down. I even entertained ideas of how much I would enjoy *owning* the *Star*, which I fully intended to do if they didn't kill that story.

Kaplan sent a limousine to meet us at the airport, and it whisked us directly to the *Star* offices in Tarrytown, New York. I remember being surprised at how unimpressive the reception area looked—it didn't fit my image of what the offices of a national tabloid news magazine should look like.

I was still feeling determined as the receptionist led us down a long hallway lined on both sides with tall file cabinets. Each drawer was labeled with some outrageous topic: abortions (did they know about mine?), political scandals, celebrity affairs, and so on. By the time we reached the conference room at the end of the hall, I was feeling somewhat shaken. It hit me, suddenly, that this time I wasn't dealing with a small-town, dickweed radio station. The *Star* may have been a supermarket tabloid, but they had a huge national circulation and a much slicker operation than I had initially given them credit for.

A massive hardwood table dominated the conference room, and the smell of ink and paper was strong. The reality of my situation was beginning to sink in—here I was, standing in a newspaper office fighting to preserve the secrecy of my affair with a man who might possibly be our next president.

A copy of the *Star* was prominently displayed at the far end of the conference table. I picked it up and gasped when I read the headline: DEM'S FRONT-RUNNER BILL CLINTON CHEATED WITH MISS AMERICA AND FOUR OTHER BEAUTIES—A FORMER MISS ARKANSAS, A SINGER, A REPORTER AND HIS OWN PRESS SPOKESWOMAN. The word "singer" jumped right out at me. I said to Blake, "Look at this. Is it real?"

With shaking hands, I opened to the story and, sure enough, there was my name right in the middle of the list: "Gennifer Flowers, a cabaret singer from Little Rock, Ark." The next page displayed the picture taken of me beside my car and a photograph of my former apartment building, the Quapaw Tower. Next to that was a picture of the apartment manager, who said in a caption that he had seen Bill visit me there ten to twenty times. My heart nearly stopped. This was worse than I ever could have imagined.

It was real, all right. Blake and I purposely laid the *Star* back on the table where we had found it, walked to the other end, and sat down. I didn't want to be gawking at it when Kaplan came through the door, because if his intention was to intimidate me with it, I needed to compose myself to avoid letting my face show he was succeeding. My confidence was fading quickly, but I still believed I held the trump card—a lawsuit.

Dick Kaplan walked into the room flanked by his attorney and carrying a tape recorder. He appeared to be in his late fifties, medium height, and somewhat heavyset. His face showed an unanticipated kindness, but that only made me more wary. I wasn't about to fall for any tricks. Kaplan placed the tape recorder on the table and started to speak. I interrupted him immediately, asking, "First of all, is that tape recorder on?" He backed off right away and said, "Oh, no, no, no. If it makes you feel better, I'll take it out of the room." Victory for Gennifer, I thought. Did he really think I would start to spill my guts into his tape recorder? Besides, for all I knew the entire room was bugged. Or maybe we were being videotaped.

Kaplan returned to the room, minus the tape recorder, and picked up the copy of the *Star* that was still lying on the table. He held it up for me to see and told me it was going to be on the newsstands in just a few days—with or without my cooperation. Indignantly, I said, "You know you can't do that. You can't print my name and my picture in there without my permission." I had played my ace in the hole, and I eagerly watched his face to see what his reaction would be.

To his credit, Kaplan didn't gloat. He gently said, "Gennifer, let me tell you how this works. As soon as Larry Nichols filed the lawsuit, anybody could print your name along with the word 'alleged.' And you don't have a basis for a lawsuit because it's public record." I was dumbfounded. I looked to Blake. I knew he would have a brilliant legal comeback to counter that statement, wouldn't he? Blake fidgeted a little and looked uncomfortable, and he wasn't saying anything. But the expression on his face told it all—Kaplan was right. My heart sank.

Then the *Star*'s attorney piped in and said the article would be all over the country by the following Tuesday, and what they wanted from me was corroboration. All this was too much for me to absorb. My heart was racing and I felt like I was backed into a corner. I told

Kaplan, "I'd like to talk to my attorney in private, please." I had to get out of there, and I felt like I was going to throw up. They showed us into another office, and I was so scared, I was sure the room was wired and they were listening to our conversation. I must have looked like the Pink Panther, sneaking around the room, looking for microphones and tape recorders. My imagination was out of control.

I brought my finger up to my lips to signal to Blake not to say anything that might be overheard, and I walked over to him and put my lips right against his ear and whispered, "Can they do this?" He whispered back glumly, "Yes, they can. You can file a lawsuit, but it's not going to stop this issue." A hundred things went through my mind as I tried to digest this astonishing news. The truth was going to come out whether I wanted it to or not. I couldn't stop it. How could I even go back to Little Rock? My apartment had been ransacked, I had lost my singing job, and my mother and I had both received threatening telephone calls. I kept thinking about the danger I was in, too. What about all those people who had been hurt or killed when they became a threat to Bill Clinton and his circle of power?

Also, this would cartainly end my romance with Finis. He would surely be uncomfortable when his fellow employees saw his girl-friend's name splashed all over the tabloids.

Reporters had already been following me everywhere, and now it would only get worse. I couldn't go back to my job at the Appeal Tribunal. How could I command respect from the two dozen employees I supervised once my affair with Bill was revealed? Plus, once everyone knew about our connection, they'd quickly figure out how I got the job in the first place. I had only about a thousand dollars in the bank and I knew no more paychecks would be coming. What could I do?

As I stood there, mind reeling, I realized the fire was out of control, and there was no escaping the flames this time. I was about to have some of the most intimate details of my life revealed to the world. Bill Clinton and I were about to become the central players in a personal and political scandal of a depth I couldn't begin to conceive. Bill couldn't help me any longer, nor could my attorney. I was painfully alone, with no control and no idea where to go or what to do.

Ten

E ver since the Bill Clinton/Gennifer Flowers story broke, the public perception has been that I smelled money, sought out the *Star*, and offered to sell them my story. Nothing could be further from the truth. Even as I sat in the *Star*'s offices, with full knowledge that their exposé was going to hit the newsstands, I was still looking for a way out. I knew I was grabbing for straws, but I'd been in a few tight positions in my life, and I could usually find a way to maneuver myself out. There *had* to be a solution to this one, too.

I felt trapped. Blake and I decided it would be best to stall for time. We returned to the conference room and I told Dick Kaplan, "I need to think about this. I have a lot to consider, a lot to think over." He agreed and suggested we go to the hotel where they had booked us rooms. So Blake and I headed for cover and a much-needed chance to think and plan. Even though I hadn't agreed to corroborate anything yet, they were panicked that some other media would get my story first. So they sent Marion Collins, a reporter, to the hotel with us, just to be sure no one approached us on the way. She was prepared to go into the bathroom with me if she felt it was necessary.

I spent the most restless night of my life. Blake and I talked for hours, I called my mother and talked at length with her, and I tried to objectively evaluate the situation as best I could. I did not call Bill. He was powerful in Arkansas, but his influence didn't reach much beyond the state line, so I really didn't think there was anything he could do. Besides, I was pretty sure any advice he might give me would be in *his* best interest, not mine.

I longed for a book of instructions to guide me through this. I had no "master plan" as I have since been accused of having, and I had no idea what my next step should be. Blake was an accomplished attorney, but he freely admitted this wasn't his field of expertise. All he could tell me was, "Do what you think is best," so I really felt I was on my own. I was flying by the seat of my pants, making all my decisions on the basis of my survival instinct.

As devastated as I was, I knew I had to summon all my emotional strength to face this squarely. I needed to think, and I had precious little time to do so. I finally decided I had two immediate goals: to become as high profile as possible to ensure my personal safety, and to do something about my financial security. Giving myself maximum visibility was crucial. As I said, people who posed a threat to Bill Clinton had a habit of ending up hurt or dead, and if I could prevent it, I wasn't about to become another statistic because of all this.

Then there was my financial situation to consider. The thousand dollars I had in the bank wasn't going to get me far, and I had no hope of getting a job anywhere once everything exploded. I had to decide quickly just what to do. I still did *not* want to do this, but I could see no way out. I decided if the *Star* would offer me money—enough money to get me out of Little Rock so I could lie low until it all blew over—I would corroborate their story. I didn't feel I had any other choice. And, after all, it was true.

I now know I *did* have another choice, and it would have been a much better one. I could have given an interview to Connie Chung or Barbara Walters—someone with the mainstream media—and signed a book deal right away. That would have accomplished both of my objectives—high visibility and financial security—with the added bonus of giving me more credibility. As fairly as the *Star* treated me, a supermarket tabloid lacks believability with the public. I think public perception of me might have been much different had I told my story in a different forum.

When Blake and I met with Dick the next morning, my first impression of his kindness returned. I fervently hoped I was right. With an air of resignation, I told him I would corroborate their story. He was pleased, and asked me a couple of questions to make sure there really was a story. First, he wanted to know just how long our relationship had gone on. When I told him it had been off and on for about twelve years, his eyes got real big.

He asked if I had any proof of our relationship. When I told him, "I have some tape-recorded phone conversations between Bill and me," his eyes nearly popped right out of his head! Not only had I been involved in a long-term relationship with Bill, but I had proof. Then came the offer. You could have knocked me over with a feather when he quoted a six figure amount! That was a lot of money for me and would lift a huge burden from my shoulders. It wasn't enough to live on for the rest of my life, but certainly enough to solve my immediate problem and give me some breathing room. Like it or not, I had to look out for myself.

The deal was made. I would corroborate the story and give them everything I could remember about my years with Bill. We started talking, going over some of the details of the relationship, and Dick decided the story should cover two issues of the *Star*. He, of course, wanted to hear the tapes, so I arranged to have them retrieved from my hiding place in Little Rock and delivered to the *Star*.

When I first arrived in New York, I was prepared to hate Dick Kaplan because of what his magazine was about to do to me, but my opinion of him was growing more favorable by the minute. There was no question that his loyalty was to the *Star* and that his interest in me was pretty much limited to getting a sensational story. But he didn't seem to be a hustler. He honestly seemed concerned about me and showed unexpected kindness toward me. All and all, I'd say he was a class act.

I had originally planned to spend one night in New York and go home the next day. Instead, I stayed almost two weeks, and Blake stayed with me. Even though he had been unable to get me out of my predicament, he was a rock of support for me when I needed one most.

Marion Collins, the reporter assigned to do my story, was a conservative British woman with brown hair and an understated style of dress. She wore little or no makeup and reminded me of the stereotypical British nanny: kindly but no-nonsense. She took up residence in the hotel where Blake and I were staying, and was by my side night and day, eking out the tiniest details, pressing me to make sure I had the chronology of events correct. She was insistent I not slip up on dates and give anyone the opportunity to discredit my story on the basis of a factual error.

At first she put me off because I thought she was being pushy. But gradually she made me realize the importance of being accurate. That was the most difficult part of the interviews. I had never kept a diary, and I never made any mental notes to the effect of "Today is September First, and Bill Clinton came to my apartment." And I had moved around a lot—from club to club and from town to town. I knew it was important to get the dates straight and not overlook anything, but it was hard sifting through twelve years of memories.

She was absolutely correct in predicting that people would be looking for the tiniest inconsistency in order to discredit the entire story. For example, I told her that Bill and I would meet at the Excelsior Hotel, among other places, when I visited him in Little Rock. But when the story was printed, it sounded as though the Excelsior was our exclusive hangout.

John Robert Starr, a columnist for the *Arkansas Democrat-Gazette*, jumped on that tidbit right away. He got a whole column out of the fact that the Excelsior hadn't even been built during some of the time I was claiming to have met Bill there. Because of that one misstatement of fact, he cast doubt on the rest of the story. He, by the way, was the columnist who claimed to have talked to each of the women in Larry Nichols' lawsuit . . . but he never even tried to contact me.

But he wasn't the only one trying to cast doubt on my credibility. The story mentioned how I had traveled with the Roy Clark Show, and some reporter decided to check up on that information. The publicist at Roy's office was new, and she told the caller she didn't know Gennifer Flowers, but would check on it. The next day's headlines were all about how Roy Clark had denied I was his back-up singer! Roy, bless his heart, later made a public statement on the *Joan Rivers Show* that I had indeed traveled with him as a back-up singer. He further said he had a lot of respect for me, which I thought took a lot of guts considering my character had been shredded to the point I was perceived as the queen of evil by then.

Marion was very nice to me, and it wasn't long before I warmed up to her. Ultimately, I developed a great respect for her ability as a reporter. She seemed to understand how difficult it was for me to reveal personal details of my relationship with Bill, and she went out of her way to make me feel comfortable. By the time we were done with the interviews, I had grown attached to her. We had spent so much time together and I had spilled my guts so thoroughly to her that she almost seemed like my personal psychiatrist.

Before the big issue of the *Star* even hit the newsstands, the national media got hold of advance copies, and the story was all over the country, seemingly within hours. The European media picked up on it, too, and were writing and broadcasting about the latest American political scandal. European newspapers were calling me the

"the most dangerous woman in America." That nickname stuck and popped up in almost every subsequent news article. Meanwhile, I was thrust into a cloak-and-dagger existence in New York.

The *Star* wouldn't let me stay in any hotel for more than a day or two, for fear some other reporter might find me. But changing hotels was an adventure in itself. I had to disguise myself with wigs and dark glasses when I went outside, and I had to register under a different false name at every hotel.

I was a wreck. This wasn't getting easier, it was just getting increasingly confusing and frightening. As much as Blake was helping me and offering emotional support, I felt cast adrift. Poor Mother was back in Missouri going crazy. I was calling her from the various hotel rooms I was in, but I was so paranoid, I wasn't certain my calls weren't being monitored. I needed someone I could trust completely there with me. So the *Star* agreed to fly Mother to New York.

I was never happier to see anyone in my life. As soon as she arrived, I collapsed with the flu. I was so beat down. I went to bed with a fever, feeling like death, and watched Bill and Hillary refute my story on *Sixty Minutes*. As soon as the first two *Star* issues came out with my story, Bill's spin doctors went to work. Bill had already vehemently denied the story, saying I had made it all up for money. My reaction to that was if it were supposedly untrue and no big deal, why were they reacting in such a big way?

As sick as I was, nothing could keep me from watching Bill and Hillary on television that night. I propped my head up on a couple of pillows and pulled the blankets up around my chin to help battle the chills I was having. The show began, and as the camera focused in on Bill, conflicting emotions bounced around inside me. In spite of everything I was going through because of him, he was still the man I had loved for many years. To see him on television with the knowledge I probably would never be able to see him face-to-face again made my heart ache.

Then the interview began. I was astonished at how lightly Steve Kroft, the *Sixty Minutes* reporter, treated Bill. Steve asked him a few pointed questions, but never tried to pin him to the mat. It was the Bill and Hillary show, all the way, and was designed to make Bill come out on the other side looking like the injured party. Bill and Hillary played the happy couple, lying through their teeth, and Steve Kroft let them get away with it.

I was seething with outrage. To watch the two of them sit there with innocent looks on their faces, lying to the entire country, was infuriating. I saw a side of Bill Clinton that night that I had never seen before, and I was disgusted. This was not the man I had fallen in love with. I didn't really expect Bill to come right out and admit he had been involved with me, but I had hoped, for his own good, he would be a little more honest with the American people and at least own up to some fooling around.

Don Hewitt, the *Sixty Minutes* executive producer, admitted later that they really weren't looking for the truth on that show. He said the purpose of that show was to get ratings. They knew they had a hot item and that the show was going to be on immediately after the Super Bowl. It was sensational and they had a built-in audience. They didn't need to do any hard investigating. And people say the *Star* lacks credibility! *Sixty Minutes* sure didn't expend any effort to interview *me*. No one called me and said they were interviewing Bill Clinton and would like to get my response. It was all hype, and Bill took advantage of every opportunity to make himself look good.

I imagined the conversation that must have taken place between Bill and Hillary, and bet Hillary did all the talking, saying, "It's going to be real hard for you to run for president while you're going through a divorce, and if you humiliate me in front of the nation, that's exactly what's going to happen. I don't give a damn what you want to do; you better deny it." And that's exactly what Bill did. I don't think he felt he had a choice but to deny it because of Hillary.

Had he been smart, he would have put it all to rest by acknowledging there had been other women, but that was in the past, their marriage was strong, and they were going forward. Bill would have been a hero! He would have created the appearance of a politician who could tell the truth, even if it was painful. People can relate to politicians being human and probably would have had a lot of respect for his honesty.

But he didn't do that. Even though he denied having an affair with me and accused me of fabricating the story for profit, he wouldn't come right out and say he had been faithful to Hillary. He left that little door open for people to doubt his honesty, and most people really did think he was being untruthful. Consequently, he has had to struggle with character issues since the beginning of his campaign, and they have only gotten worse as the years pass. It was a calculated political move on his part to deny, but be evasive, and I think whoever persuaded him to handle it that way gave him bad advice.

Watching *Sixty Minutes* that night, intellectually I understood what Bill was trying to do. I knew Hillary had more than a little influence over the things he said, and I also knew he was desperately trying to salvage his campaign. My emotional reaction, however, was a little different. I thought he was a son of a bitch. What a crummy thing to do. I wasn't the one lying—Bill was. I hadn't asked to be in the public spotlight—Bill had. I had been unwillingly stripped naked for the world to examine, and dismissed as unworthy, and Bill was the catalyst for that dismissal. The emotional pain that resulted from seeing Bill on *Sixty Minutes* was some of the worst I had ever experienced.

Not only did he betray me, but he also *continued* to betray me by organizing a massive character assassination that went full-steam ahead from that day forward. He knew I wasn't a bad person. If I were, if my motivation had been to plot against him, I could have had his butt in a sling long before then. When he waged an all-out campaign to discredit me and shred my character, he knew what his people were doing to me, and he let it happen. He may have felt bad about it to some degree, but he wasn't willing to stop it. He left me dangling in the wind in an impossible situation.

I was devastated. I had really hit rock bottom. I took measure of what I had gained and what I had lost, and what I had lost seemed much larger at that point. I had achieved my goals of high visibility and financial security, but my lover of twelve years had denied me to the world and dismissed me as a gold-digger. All we had shared was rendered meaningless, and all our beautiful memories were tarnished when he so casually tossed me to the wolves.

Immediately after the *Sixty Minutes* interview with Bill and Hillary, the *Star* people came to me and said, "You have to do a press conference." I was still sick in bed, I could hardly lift my head, and they were telling me I had to hold a press conference. All I really wanted to do was go home, crawl in bed, and pull the covers up over my head. This wasn't what I had anticipated, and I wanted it to be over.

But they told me because Bill had denied our relationship, I had to go in front of the public and establish my credibility. I had to let people see and hear me, let them know I wasn't some monster. Their plan was to play a few excerpts from the tapes to let people hear for themselves that it was, indeed, Bill Clinton speaking. I was too sick to argue, and thought it best to take their advice. I couldn't remember ever being in such a low emotional state, but I wasn't ready to roll over and die either. If there was something I could do to make myself believable, I was more than willing to do it. Through the haze of fever, I realized the *Star* had an additional motive in putting me in front of news cameras: capitalizing on Bill and Hillary's television appearance would only sell more magazines. I didn't care about that, though, I just wanted to be believed.

The *Star* people talked with me a little bit, trying to determine what points to make at the press conference. Then they helped me prepare a statement. Even though the statement was based on my thoughts, it came out much stronger than I had intended.

Blake and I were picked up the next day in Connecticut, where we were staying by then, by a beautiful white limousine filled with lawyers and staff members from the *Star*, and taken to the Waldorf Astoria Hotel in New York. The *Star* had rented the ballroom, and it was jam-packed with television, radio, and magazine reporters from all over the world. The camera people were stacked ten deep in front of the stage. Fortunately, the *Star* had arranged for a strong security force, and I was grateful. I was completely overwhelmed by the number of reporters there. It was hard to imagine that all those people were interested in *me*. A *Star* executive told me later that he hadn't seen a press conference that large for anyone besides George Bush, the president of the United States.

Blake made a few opening remarks, addressing some items reported in the *Star* article that had been questioned, trying to clear up any discrepancies. Then I got up and read my statement, and a few excerpts from the tapes were played. I was feeling much better but was still weak from the flu. Had I been physically strong, I think I would have been psychologically stronger, too. But as it was, I felt almost removed from the scene, like an out-of-body experience. I didn't have the tiniest clue what was going to happen, and didn't really care a whole lot.

After I completed my statement, I took questions from the press. One reporter asked about my state job, but I couldn't give him a lengthy answer because it was just too complicated. I knew that the full story of how I got my state job would be covered in detail in the final *Star* issue of my story, which would be coming out the following week. So I told him his question would be answered then.

They asked if I was afraid of Bill Clinton, if I was trying to disqualify him from the White House, and if I was trying to set him up when I taped the calls. They were tough questions, but I tried to answer as honestly as I could.

Then from the crowd of reporters came a loud voice asking if Bill used a condom when we had sex. I found out later he was "Stuttering John" Melendez from the Howard Stern Show, who made a career of asking outrageous questions. But I didn't know that at the time, and I thought, "Oh great, here we go." I have to admit, I was chuckling inside, because I couldn't believe he had the guts to ask that question. But I kept a straight face, and Blake told the crowd if there were any more degrading questions, the press conference would be over.

From that moment on, most reporters asked very serious, insightful questions. I thought the press conference was actually going pretty well. The questions were getting tougher, though. I was asked if Bill had ever advised me to just tell the truth (which he hadn't) and if I had ever been approached by the Republican Party (which I had). The question that touched me the most was from a reporter who asked if Bill's denial of our relationship hurt me. Just hearing that question gave my heart a turn, and I answered softly, "Yes, very much."

We had been advised by the *Star* to try to avoid women reporters. They said women tended to be more judgmental with their questions. But I had noticed a woman standing in the group, nicely dressed, very well groomed, and smiling sweetly at me. Blake was choosing reporters to ask questions, so I whispered to him to select her as the next questioner. Big mistake! She asked me one of the meanest and most insulting questions of the entire press conference. She asked me if I felt sleazy for having taped the conversations. I answered her, saying I did not feel sleazy, but I thought, "Gennifer, you buffoon. She really took you in." Little did I know, she wasn't going to be the last one to take me in. That was the first indication to me of how my taping our conversations was going to be perceived by a large percentage of the public—not as self-protection, but as "sleazy."

Just like that it was over. I was surrounded by security people hustling me out, and as we neared the exit, a photographer got a little too close. Without warning, he was slammed up against the wall by a security guard. Once again, my mind had trouble acknowledging that I was at the center of all the commotion.

Riding back to the hotel, the intensity and the seriousness of the events of the day really started to sink in. This was a major event in the world right then, and there was little ol' me right in the middle of it. I couldn't believe this was happening to me. Was I doing the right thing? Was I being used? What did Bill think of all this? What was I doing?

I wouldn't let Mother go with me to the press conference. I didn't know what to expect, and I just didn't want her to get caught up in anything ugly. So she stayed at the hotel in Connecticut, nervously watching the press conference on TV, and when I got back, she grabbed on to me and wouldn't let go. Our hotel room *du jour* had two bedrooms, and both CNN and the New York local news had carried the press conference live. Mother had run from one bedroom to the next, watching both stations, trying to get every detail, all the while worried to death about her little girl.

When I finally found a quiet moment that evening, I reflected on the events of the previous few days. It all could have turned out so differently. I wish I would have had the opportunity to give Bill some advice about the whole situation. In the past, I had often advised him when he was in a sticky mess, and, more often than not, he took my advice. When he made an idiot of himself at the Democratic convention in the summer of 1988 with a speech that dragged on forever and just about put the crowd to sleep, he called me. He was distraught and angry. He believed he had been set up by Michael Dukakis' people because they considered Bill a potential candidate who might one day oppose Dukakis, and they wanted to make him look bad. So they gave him that horrible speech to read, and the crowd cheered when he finally shut up.

He had gotten an offer to appear on *The Tonight Show*, but he didn't want to do it. He felt he already looked enough like a monkey and didn't want to make it any worse. I told him, "If you've got any sense at all, you'll do it. Go on there and let people see you as a person. Just be yourself and dispel all this crap." That's exactly what he did. He went on the show, played his saxophone, let Johnny Carson poke fun at him, and he laughed at himself. The criticism about his speech died out right away.

Had I been given the opportunity to advise Bill about the exposure of our affair, I would have told him to go before the American people and tell them the truth. At least then people could have made up their minds about him on the basis of their personal convictions, not on whether or not they thought he was a liar.

News of our relationship would have flared up and died out in the blink of an eye had he just owned up to it and moved on. But he had to lie. And that set us both on a long, twisted path that would keep our affair in the public eye and make it part of history.

I had many thoughts that evening after the press conference. But my greatest wish was to pack my bags and get out of New York. I was totally drained, emotionally and physically. I was sick, tired, and scared, and all I wanted to do was take the money I had gotten for the story, go someplace, and be anonymous. I wanted to start my life over as best I could. I had no intention of doing anything else with the media—I just wanted to go away and be left alone. But, it wasn't to be.

Eleven

I hadn't called Finis to forewarn him about the *Star* story before it hit the newsstands. He saw it, of course, along with the televised press conference, and called all over New York looking for me. I didn't call him until after I got back to Little Rock, and he was going out of his mind with worry. It pleased me to know that even though our relationship was on ice, I could still count on him to be a source of strength.

He never came right out and said he couldn't handle it anymore and didn't want to see me. He didn't have to; I knew it intuitively. I was heartbroken and hated the thought of losing the only man who was wonderful enough to pry me away from Bill Clinton. In the back of my mind I held out some hope that maybe I could salvage our relationship, but I also knew it was going to take all my emotional energy just to survive. Every ounce of strength had to be put into dealing with my situation. I had to let go of Finis.

I couldn't be with him and pretend everything was the way it used to be, and he couldn't look at me the same way, either. I hoped I could trust him and that he would always be there for me, but it wasn't fair to pull him into my own personal whirlpool of controversy. Without ever speaking the words, our plans for a life together melted away. We kept in touch, and I never doubted Finis cared about me, but the relationship we had shared before I went to New York was over.

Even though I grew up in Arkansas, I had no inkling of what was in store for me when I got back to Little Rock. The power structure in Arkansas continues to amaze me to this day. The local media picked on Bill, but they didn't like it when someone from outside their little group criticized him. The national media was brutal with the local boys. They couldn't understand why Arkansas had this story about Larry Nichols' lawsuit all along but never went anywhere with it.

What the national media didn't understand was Bill could have gotten away with just about anything in Arkansas. The good ol' boy system was more concerned with what Bill could do for them than what they could do to Bill. The worldwide press made Arkansas journalists look like idiots for sitting on the story. They had egg all over their faces, and they took it out on me.

Arkansas was my home. I may not have been a nationally known politician, but I had accomplished a lot in the entertainment business and was a source of pride for Arkansas. Many newspaper articles were written praising my achievements in the entertainment business. But the newspapers turned on me like barracudas when the outside media made them look incompetent. Before I even got back to Little Rock, the local newspapers had launched a campaign to discredit me.

As Blake and I headed back to Little Rock, I thought about how I needed a few days to pack up and decide where to go, and I hoped I could do so with a minimum of attention. We had to change planes halfway to Little Rock, and while we were waiting for our flight, Blake went to get a magazine. I was seated in the terminal and could see people looking at me and whispering. My face was plastered all over the news by this time, and people were recognizing me.

As I waited for Blake to come back, a man walked by me, turned around, glared at me, and said, "I hope they paid you enough." I pretended not to hear him, but a chill went through my body. I was further dismayed when I saw him get on our same flight to Little Rock. Blake returned, and I told him what had happened. He told me not to worry, the *Star* had provided us with first class tickets, so we weren't likely to run into him again.

After we were seated on the plane, I told Blake, "I guarantee you, before this flight's over, he'll walk up here." Sure enough, before we landed, he walked up to first class, used the rest room, and as he walked back down the aisle, he glared at me again. This wasn't a good start, and it scared me.

We landed in Little Rock, and because no one knew we were coming, no reporters were at the airport. I got to my apartment, and Blake helped me with my bags, then left me on my own. It was the first time in two weeks I had been alone, and for a few moments I enjoyed the silence. But no more than ten minutes had passed when someone knocked on the door. I peered out through the peephole but couldn't tell if the person standing at the door was a reporter. The thought wasn't too far from my mind that it could very well be someone who meant me physical harm.

Needless to say, I didn't answer the door. I peeked out through the drapes occasionally, and people were starting to gather. Word was getting around: I was home. Most of them had cameras, but I actually felt a little reassured thinking that even though I wasn't anxious to have a lot of reporters around, at least there was safety in numbers. The Arkansas press could do whatever they wanted to me, but I wasn't anxious to tangle with any of Bill's boys.

Then my telephone rang. I jumped a foot and just stared at it. I wouldn't answer it, but as soon as it stopped ringing, it would start up again. It was more than a little unnerving. In between calls, I grabbed the phone and frantically dialed a friend. I begged her to come get me—I had to get out of there. My apartment had a picture window that looked out on the front, but my doorway was in back, off a hallway. I noticed that the reporters seemed to congregate on one side of the building, so I told my friend to come in on the quiet side, and we could try to slip out through the back.

How we managed to avoid the reporters, I haven't a clue. But we missed them all. When she brought me home later, it was the same routine. I got back inside without encountering anyone, but within ten seconds, the knocking started again. Either they were very stupid, or I was very lucky.

Mother wanted to come to Little Rock to help me move, but I wasn't about to put her in any danger or subject her to all those crazy reporters. I called my dear friend, Margie Moore, whom I had met while we both were working at the Cipango Club in Dallas. Margie sang in the lounge at the Cipango for thirty-four years, and we became close friends almost as soon as we met. She is a lovely, petite Italian woman with brown hair, brown eyes, and a gentle smile. We had maintained frequent contact no matter where I was living and working.

Margie was still in Dallas, and when I talked to her on the telephone she urged me to move back. "You still have friends in Dallas, kid," she told me. Margie had been called by dozens of reporters and interviewed by *Inside Edition*, but the interview was never aired, presumably because it put me in a positive light.

Margie had known about Bill and me and was eager to lend a supportive hand. I thought about it for maybe ten seconds before I decided Dallas was where I would go. There was no possibility of staying in Little Rock unless I wanted to hibernate until the election was over. That wasn't very appealing, and I had difficulty believing I could pull it off in the first place. I made up my mind to go to Dallas right away and find a place to live. I caught a plane, and Margie picked me up at the airport. It took us one day to find an apartment and buy a new car.

The car I already had was still sitting in the garage of my apartment building in Little Rock. It had been there the entire two weeks I was in New York, and the garage was easily accessible to anyone who wanted to get in. There was nothing in the world that could induce me to get in that car and start it up. I was painfully aware that I was not a popular lady in Arkansas by that time. And Bill had a multitude of hangers on who wouldn't hesitate to do anything if they thought it might help him. Every time I thought about starting my car, I would picture a huge explosion.

I had a friend named Tanya in Little Rock who was really struggling. She had three children and received little or no child support. I was amazed at how she worked two or three jobs at a time to support her kids. She would literally go from job to job to job, just to put food on the table. I called her and said, "Look, I want to level with you. I am not sure there isn't a bomb in my car. I'm afraid to start it or even touch it for that matter. But if you've got the guts to start it, it's yours."

My car was a little Mazda RX-7, several years old but in perfect condition. It was a good car, and I knew it would help her out a lot to have a car for her teenage son. There was no way she could afford to buy one. Tanya thought about it for maybe two seconds, and said, "I'll take the chance." I immediately regretted the offer. I told her, "Please understand, I care about you, and this could be it!" She told me not to worry, she'd bring her son and her dad, and they would check it out thoroughly. Her dad, she told me, knew a lot about cars and would be able to spot anything amiss.

Margie drove back to Little Rock with me in my new car, and I called Tanya and asked if she was still interested in the Mazda. She was, and came to the garage with her son and father. I was shaking like a leaf, and feeling kind of funny about dragging her into my deal. I said, "Now, Tanya, I mean it. I'm not standing close to this car while you're trying to start it." But her dad and her son had carefully inspected it, didn't find a thing unusual, and she was ready to start it up.

Margie and I huddled together like chickens at the far end of the garage, expecting the worst. I felt like a murderer and wished I had kept my mouth shut. If anything happened to Tanya, it would be my fault. Tanya got in, turned the key, and it wouldn't start—wouldn't start—wouldn't start; and finally it turned over. The engine roared to life. No bomb! I was shaking with relief! Tanya had her car, was safe, and I had one less thing to worry about.

I kept trying to tell myself that I was letting unreasonable fears take over my better sense, but even today, as I look back, I know that wasn't the case. The fear I experienced was legitimate. Too many bad, and sometimes fatal things had happened to people who dared to cross Bill Clinton. And I had crossed him in the worst possible way: I was threatening to bring down his candidacy for the president of the United States. A lot of people in Arkansas wanted very badly for Bill to be president. It's hard to predict what a sick or overly ambitious mind might think up.

Margie and I were packing a few things to take back to Dallas, and, as usual, the phone was ringing off the wall. Margie decided to have some fun, and she answered one of the calls. Someone named Rusty was calling from Nashville and wanted to put together a record deal with me. In fun, Margie told him she had just gotten that telephone number a few days earlier, and Rusty gasped, "Do you know whose number you have?" Margie said, "Why, no, I don't." "Do you know that little filly who was involved with Bill Clinton?" Rusty asked. Margie got a good laugh out of that—I'm glad someone did. I wasn't about to answer the telephone.

★ ★ ★ ★

Blake and several of my friends had talked to me about going on television at least once so people could see me in person instead of just reading about me in the newspaper. So just before leaving Little Rock, I agreed to appear on *A Current Affair*. The reason I chose that particular show was simple: they offered me the most money. I wasn't crazy about the idea of doing the show, but I relied on the advice of my attorney and my friends. And if they felt I should do it, then I was going to make damn sure I was well compensated for it.

After all I had been through, I was feeling less and less guilty about being paid for talking about my relationship with Bill. My attitude had definitely changed, and for that I offer my deepest apologies to the American people. It was not my original intent to capitalize on my notoriety. But I had been called names, criticized, vilified, and ridiculed, all for telling the truth. And since the media made money off my story, why shouldn't I?

Maureen O'Boyle conducted the interview for *A Current Affair*, and she went fairly easy on me. She pressed me a little on the content of the tapes, asking me why the conversation wasn't sexier if Bill and I were supposed to be lovers. I told her that our relationship had ended nearly two years before the tapes were made, and it would have been inappropriate for us to have had an intimate conversation at that time. She tried to trip me up on a few details, but backed off quickly when she wasn't able to.

I was pleased *A Current Affair* treated me as a human being talking about a hurtful situation rather than as a scheming opportunist. I wasn't sure how it would turn out, though, while we were taping the interview. When we would take a break for a few minutes, Steve Dunleavy, a show executive, would huddle with Maureen, and I would secretively confer with Blake. It reminded me of fighters in a ring, each going to his corner between rounds to get advice and encouragement. When we resumed the interview, Maureen would be all charged up and try to maneuver me into a corner, but again, she wasn't able to do it.

With my appearance on *A Current Affair* behind me, I headed for my new home. I had called a mover to come pack the rest of my belongings and move everything to Dallas. I gave strict instructions not to speak to the media. But the reporters wouldn't leave those poor movers alone, trying to get any piece of information they could about where I was going. The movers had an extremely difficult time loading the truck. But they finally managed to get everything loaded, escape the reporters, and head to Dallas.

Even though I breathed a sigh a relief to be out of Little Rock and to have regained a little bit of privacy, I felt kind of sad, too. I had virtually been driven out of town under a black cloud, and I wasn't happy about that. My immediate plans were to get settled, then do what I had always done: get back into the entertainment business. I really thought my time in the spotlight was over and I could get back to life as usual.

Once again, wishful thinking.

After the movers delivered my things in Dallas, I set about unpacking and arranging furniture. As haphazard as my packing and the move had been, I expected to be missing any number of possessions. But there was only one box missing, and, coincidentally, it was the box that contained the little twenty dollar tape recorder I had used to tape my conversations with Bill.

I hadn't completely recovered from the flu I had while I was in New York, and I had started coughing again while Margie and I were packing my things in Little Rock. I was trying to get organized in Dallas, but I was feeling worse and worse. I finally reached the point where I had so little strength, I couldn't even lift a box. I went to the doctor and he quickly diagnosed me with pneumonia.

He prescribed vitamins and antibiotics, but also told me I had to go to bed until the pneumonia went away. I had been under so much emotional stress from the events of the past few weeks and under so much physical stress from the flu that hadn't gone away, I was in bad shape. There I was in my new apartment, with boxes stacked to the ceiling, and I had to go to bed.

It took three months before I was completely recovered, and not a peaceful three months, either. Blake was calling me constantly with offers from the media. Everyone wanted to do a story or an interview with Gennifer Flowers. All the talk shows wanted me, the European media was after me, and I just wanted to be left alone. Blake was really getting into the swing of things, however. No one knew how to find me, thank God, but he was getting hundreds of calls and was thrust into the position of acting as my agent.

Once I did *A Current Affair*, I had intended to retire from the public eye for awhile, but it just wasn't working. While I was in bed with pneumonia, Bill Clinton and his campaign workers continued their offensive against Gennifer Flowers that left me stunned. Twenty or thirty other women came forward during this time saying they had had an involvement with Bill. His aide, Betsey Wright, coined the phrase "The Bimbo Eruption" to describe the other women . . . and it spread like wildfire. And guess who was named the head bimbo?

I was vilified for having had an affair with a married man. I freely admit I'm no saint, and I have never tried to justify or excuse my behavior. But from all the finger pointing and accusations, you would think I was the first woman ever to get involved with a married man. Somehow the whole, sordid mess became *my* fault, and Bill was just an innocent victim. Being called a bimbo stirred up a volcano of anger in me. Yes, I had an affair with a married man. Yes, it was the wrong thing to do, and I have spent a lot of time over the past few years asking God for forgiveness. But to be dismissed as a bimbo because of my bad judgment in one area of my life was more than I could ignore. The volcano was about to erupt.

I knew it was all political maneuvering on Bill's part, and game-playing on the part of the media. But it was infuriating. I was painted as a blonde, airheaded, gold-digger, and Bill was coming out of it smelling like a rose. The media sided with him. And all I had done was tell the truth and offer the only proof. Of all the women who came forward with allegations of involvement with Bill, I was the only one with any real proof, and it still wasn't good enough.

Bill had always maintained he was bulletproof. And, to a large degree, he was right. The Republicans were handed that election on a plate, and they screwed it up. It astonished me that Bill was able to survive all the revelations about his womanizing and draft dodging and still win the election. He wasn't even the Democratic front-runner when my story broke; Bob Kerrey and Paul Tsongas were both ahead of him.

Linda Bloodworth-Thomasen, Bill's friend from Arkansas who now is a Hollywood television producer, explained it best. A magazine article quoted her as saying she knew as soon as my story came out that Bill would be elected president. She could appreciate the value of publicity, whether it's positive or negative.

More power to Bill, I thought. If he could turn negative publicity into something positive for his campaign, why not? I just resented being run over as part of his strategy. The Clinton campaign staff went so far as to hire a private investigator, Jack Palladino, to investigate my background. I found this out from friends and relatives who called to tell me he had approached them with a lot of questions about me. He went all over the country looking for dirt on me. If I had ever so much as kicked a dog, he would have found out about it.

As much as I resented having my character and credibility trashed, the idea that campaign dollars might be paying for it sickened me.

Though I knew I was alone against a powerful machine, my determination to establish my credibility was growing. After all, I had the truth on my side—Bill was the one who was lying, not me. I decided to release the tapes, thinking if people could hear Bill's voice plotting to cover up and use me as a pawn, they would have to believe

I was telling the truth. The *Star* had printed excerpts from the tapes in their articles, but few people had ever had the opportunity to actually hear Bill Clinton's voice scheming to save his political rear end.

I knew, too, that not one time on the tapes did Bill worry about how any scandal might affect his family. He never expressed any concern about what it might do to his wife or his child, or even to me for that matter. He was concerned only with how he could protect himself, how he could cover himself. I decided the American public needed to hear this.

I planned to subscribe to a 900 number so the public could call and hear the tapes. I intended to charge only as much as it would cost to cover my expenses. I have no aversion to making money, but that was not my goal in doing this. My representatives contacted AT&T, and we were in the process of getting it set up, when I was attacked from all sides. First, AT&T turned me down with no explanation.

Then I heard from a group of Republicans who offered to buy the tapes from me for $900,000. They would run them, keep whatever revenue they generated, and, with any luck, fatally damage Bill Clinton's candidacy. Nine hundred thousand dollars! That was a ton of money, but, even so, I quickly vetoed that idea. It was not my intention to have the tapes used as a Republican tool. This was not a vendetta against Bill; it was my personal quest for vindication. I also didn't trust the Republicans to not doctor the tapes to make them fit their own purposes. I knew I needed to maintain control of the tapes.

Finally, the Democrats chimed in, claiming I would be violating fair campaign practices by releasing the tapes, and threatening me if I did so. I knew there was no way anyone could stop me from releasing them, threats or no threats, but it got so complicated I decided to not do it. I desperately wanted to clear my name, but I could see that I would run into so many roadblocks, my situation could actually get worse. I was smart enough to realize I was outnumbered and it might be a good time to retreat and regroup. The tapes were safe, and I could always release them at a later date. I didn't especially care *when* I cleared my name just so long as it could be accomplished eventually.

Meanwhile, it was starting to sink in that I was not going to get my life back. Having pneumonia for three months prevented me from even considering a singing job, and the unrelenting media attention didn't help either. Things might have settled down a little had I not been so determined to get a fair hearing. My anger at the gross inequities thrown my way prevented me from just lying down on the railroad tracks and letting the train run over me. I'm a fighter, and this was one of the biggest fights of my life. I wasn't about to let people think badly of me without doing everything I could to help them reach an informed opinion.

November 7, 1992 was Election Day. I had a fairly serious interest in the results of the election that year. I went to the polls with my decision made and voted for Ross Perot because by now I believed that Bill's vengeance toward me and the deception on his part could affect the whole country. I did not believe he was qualified to be president of the United States. And, like many other Americans, I felt we didn't need another four years of George Bush.

I was watching the returns on television when Finis called me from Little Rock. He was at the Excelsior Hotel, which was teeming with Bill's supporters. Finis' words burned into my ear: "Well, he's been elected." It was no surprise, of course, but I was apprehensive.

What would happen to me now?

It quickly became apparent that certain members of the media were not yet through with me. Inauguration Day presented a great opportunity in the eyes of many media types. I received offers worth probably twenty thousand dollars or more to do all kinds of things. One group wanted me to critique Hillary's wardrobe; another asked me to sing at a club in Chicago on that day; plus I had offers to do personal interviews on radio stations. But I just wasn't interested; I turned them all down.

Even after all I had been through, I wanted to let Bill and Hillary have their day. It was also a day for the citizens of America to feel hopeful. I had no desire to position myself as a vindictive woman on that day. Everything I did was perceived as a jab at Bill Clinton, and I didn't want any part of that on Inauguration Day. I wanted the country to feel good, at least for that one day, because I doubted the people of America would feel good about Bill Clinton as their president for very long.

Twelve

Several months before the election took place, the telephone rang one day while I was lying in bed recovering from my battle with pneumonia. Blake Hendrix was still serving as my attorney/agent, and he had just received an interesting offer. *Playboy* magazine wanted to do a photo layout and article about me. My initial reaction was negative—I really wasn't interested at all. But Blake persisted, "You need to know, this deal could be worth about a million dollars." That caught my attention.

This was something I had never even given a passing thought to. Magazines like *Playboy* and *Penthouse* didn't offend me, and I firmly believe women have the right to do whatever they wish with regard to nude photography. But it was never an option for me or something I aspired to even in my wildest dreams. The prospect of a million dollars, however, made me look at it from a different perspective. I had been offered nearly that much by the Republicans when they wanted to buy my tapes, but I refused to let those tapes be used in ways I couldn't control.

This was different, though. I was reasonably certain I could manage a *Playboy* photo layout with a minimum of difficulty. Blake and I had barely started talking about it when *Penthouse* entered the picture and started a bidding war with *Playboy*. *Penthouse* was offering an even more substantial package: a large sum up front, and part of the proceeds from the actual sales of the magazine. I was told the earning potential could be as high as ten million dollars. That kind of money was beyond my most optimistic expectations and was too seductive to turn down. My financial security would be guaranteed for life, and there would be a bonus: my story would be told in a way that wasn't sensational or muck-raking.

Bob Guccione, the publisher of *Penthouse*, absolutely wooed me. He assured me, "This will be about you. Bill Clinton will be in it, of course, but it will be a love story." He went on to say many actresses and other entertainers had posed for *Penthouse* or *Playboy* to further their careers: Kim Basinger and Sharon Stone, for example. He went on and on about how a nude pictorial of me would be a thing of beauty; I would be proud of it. Guccione's favorite line was, "Be a part of our *Penthouse* family." That didn't paint a particularly pretty picture in my mind, but ten million dollars was a powerful incentive to keep my opinions to myself. I would be set free financially.

Playboy wouldn't match *Penthouse*'s offer, so I was eager and ready to sign a deal with Bob Guccione. Blake had met with Victor Kovner, *Penthouse*'s lawyer, and Blake realized he was way out of his league. Blake's expertise was in criminal law, not entertainment law, so he suggested I find a representative more experienced in matters of that nature, as he didn't feel didn't able to adequately represent me in dealings with *Penthouse*. He had been an exceptionally good friend and adviser to me throughout the ordeal, and I appreciated his honesty.

After considering a couple of people who turned out to be inept, a friend suggested I talk with Roy True, who had been Mickey Mantle's business manager for twenty-five years. When I met with him, I liked him and decided to hire him. Roy was in his late fifties at the time and very distinguished looking, with white hair and pretty blue eyes. He was part of a well-respected Dallas firm, and I could tell immediately that he was an intelligent man. Plus, the chemistry between us felt good. He had a lot of experience with contract negotiations and I felt he was the right person to handle the *Penthouse* deal for me.

We negotiated the deal, and even though I was apprehensive about posing nude, the prospect of having an article written that would tell *my* side of the story for a change was very exciting. I was also breathing a huge sigh of relief over the promise of never having to worry about money again.

My contract didn't specify exactly how much money I would receive, aside from the amount paid to me up front. But Guccione gave me lots of examples of other women who had a lot of notoriety, like me, and how they had ultimately profited. He threw a lot of numbers at me: so many magazines sold would translate into so many dollars. And I was truly overwhelmed. If only half his predictions came true, five million dollars was certainly more than enough to give me security for life.

The magazine assigned Art Harris to write the article. I had never heard of him, nor had I read anything he had written, but I was assured he was the perfect person to write my love story. Art cut an imposing figure with his shaved head and steely, penetrating eyes, but he had a gentle manner. His voice was soft, and he was generously flattering. It was important that he gain my confidence, and he was skilled in doing so. He made me feel secure that he was going to write the story in the way it had been promised. He asked for a list of people whom I had known for years or who had been involved in my life, so he could develop my background and gain insight into my personality. After he interviewed me extensively, he called or met with many old friends and family members, gathering information and opinion.

Warning flags went up, however, when all those people, one by one, called to tell me Art Harris was no friend of mine. They complained he was trying to put words into their mouths, trying to get them to say things that weren't true. No one liked him, and no one trusted him.

These reports were making me extremely nervous, and I became downright agitated when I learned he was working with Jack Palladino, the private investigator hired by the Clinton campaign to unearth damaging information on me. I called Jane Hamish, Bob Guccione's personal assistant, and told her, "I don't like this guy. I have a real bad feeling about him."

Jane tried to calm my fears by explaining that Art Harris was simply caught up in his assignment. She went on to say he always got very involved in whatever his subject was and he was probably just being a little too aggressive. My worry level increased, though, when she said, "We probably should have gotten somebody else who would have been better to do this than he, because he's an investigative reporter." But she tried to reassure me. "Don't worry," she said, "we'll edit the story."

Before I'd agreed to do the *Penthouse* piece, I had made an agreement with Guccione that specified I had a right to review and approve the article and pictorial before they were published. So even though I was concerned Art Harris might be doing a hatchet job on me, I knew I could demand it be rewritten before it went to print. So I tried to put my fears at rest, blaming my anxiety on my wholesale trashing by the media. After all, I reasoned, *Penthouse* had sought me out. They were the ones who came to me wanting to do an objective and sensitive article. I really had no reason to mistrust them.

I shifted my focus to the photo shoot that was looming ahead. I had to get it over with, so I flew to Los Angeles, alone. *Penthouse* sent a car to pick me up at the airport, and I went directly to the hotel, where I was to meet Earl Miller, the photographer assigned to my pictorial.

I had talked to Earl on the telephone a few times, and he seemed like a nice man, but I was still a little wary of meeting him. We rendezvoused at the front desk of the hotel, and I was immediately impressed by his easy-going, unimposing appearance. He had that California look—jacket with the sleeves pushed up—and seemed relaxed and friendly.

We went immediately to my room, where he was planning to get an idea of what my body was like so he could prepare for the photo session. I had brought a few articles of clothing with me I thought we might possibly use during the shoot, and he asked me to put them on. I knew I had to comply, but I was a bundle of nerves.

I'm very shy with my body; I always have been. I may show a little cleavage on occasion, but I've never been one to expose a lot of skin when I dress. I'm aware of what my best features are, and I'm not likely to flaunt the parts that aren't great. My grandmother used to say, "If it doesn't look good, don't set it out on the front porch." I was a little concerned, too, because I had heard all kinds of wild stories about skin magazines and the men who put them together. I had never done anything like this before and just didn't know what to expect.

I retreated to the bathroom, dreading what I had to do, but determined to go through with it. I put on a little lace teddy, stood there for a moment gathering my courage, and timidly emerged for Earl's inspection. He had a studious, thoughtful look on his face, and didn't seem at all moved by the fact that a total stranger was standing in front of him in her underwear. To my delight, he couldn't have been more professional. He truly only wanted to see what he was going to have to deal with and what he would have to do to make me look good in the photos. As he scrutinized me, he told me he was trying to determine how he would use clothes, lighting, and positioning to my benefit. He also thought out loud about what props he might need to get for the shoot.

Earl had me do one or two turns for him, and, to my relief, that was it. I couldn't help thinking how differently he reacted to me standing there in my sheer teddy compared to the way Bill had always reacted. Earl was pure professional, while Bill had always been so excited and approving.

I went back into the bathroom, got dressed, and then we sat and talked for awhile. He talked about his wife, Margo Adams, who had been involved with Wade Boggs, the baseball player, and had gotten a lot of media attention because of it. Earl knew I could relate to her experience and generously suggested I talk with her before I left L.A. She had done a pictorial for *Penthouse* when her affair with Wade was splashed all over the newspapers and television, and Earl met her during the photo shoot.

Earl was well into his fifties when he married the first time, and he and Margo had a new baby boy. Gradually I became very comfortable with him because he was so obviously enthusiastic about his marriage and his young son. By the time he left, I was relaxed and much less apprehensive about the next day's photo shoot.

Bright and early the next morning, Earl and I went to a costume company to see what we could find to use for the photo shoot. We would be doing the shoot in a gorgeous, contemporary mansion rented exclusively for the occasion, about an hour or so outside Los Angeles. We picked out all kinds of different costumes—from medieval dresses to seductive and flimsy nightgowns—and gathered up lots of feather boas and lace accessories. Wardrobe in tow, we drove out to the mansion.

Just a few people were there waiting for us: Earl's assistant, a man to help with the sets, and the makeup and hair person. But, again, I was developing a case of nerves. As comfortable as I had become with Earl, and as much as I was trying to keep my anxiety in check, I couldn't help having reservations about this adventure. I was about to take my clothes off in front of a camera! And the resulting pictures would be printed in an internationally published magazine! I still wanted to do it, I just wished the photo session were over.

Deliberately forcing the nervousness into the back of my mind, I focused on the task ahead. I was willing to expose myself, literally, but I was also determined that if anything seemed odd, or if even one weird statement was made, I would march right out the door. I simply would not put up with it. I knew we were an hour out of town, but I would hitchhike back if I had to.

To my relief, nothing inappropriate ever happened. The makeup person was very talented both with makeup and hair, and she was sweet as could be. She and Earl were the only people present while the shots were taken. When Earl needed another camera, his assistant would come into the room, hand it to him, and leave. He kept his head averted and would not stare or even look at me. I thought that showed a lot of respect and consideration, and I was becoming increasingly comfortable with the whole program.

Earl couldn't have cared less if I was dressed or stark naked, as long as the lighting was right and he was delivering an artistic product. He had been working at *Penthouse* for nineteen years and had seen too many boobs in his career to care about yet another set. At first I was grateful for that, but as I became more at ease with him, it almost annoyed me a little!

During the first part of the shoot, I was wearing a beautiful velvet gown that looked like it was straight out of Camelot. Earl positioned me on a large staircase, and I felt very regal and queenlike. He took several pictures, and I thought, "This is easy, I can do this." Of course, I was still fully clothed.

Earl had told me not to wear any underwear, which was okay for the moment, because nothing was showing. But when he said, "I want you to pull your skirt up in front," I froze. I said no. He asked me again to pull up my skirt, and I said no again. I was overcome with shyness, and there was no way I could pull my dress up and let him see "the precious." I was beginning to think maybe I couldn't do this after all. But Earl was very patient. He talked to me for a minute or two, then said, "Gennifer, it's just me, and I don't care. Pull it up just a little."

So I lifted my skirt just a bit, not revealing much of anything, and Earl took some shots. Then he gradually had me lift it higher and higher, until I was revealing a lot. But as we went along it got easier, and then I got into the swing of things. Once I did it one time, the next time wasn't so hard.

I didn't do any shots where I was completely naked, except in the bathtub, surrounded by bubbles. I don't think I could have done anything where I was standing there completely exposed.

We shot photographs for four days, six or seven hours a day. After the first few hours all nerves were gone, and it was just hard work. The situation had become so academic by the third day, I was no longer shy and decided to have some fun. I was determined to make Earl notice me. Well, he did! Earl had me positioned on a stairway landing, dressed in a cape that flowed down from my head around my shoulders, but left my breasts exposed. I was holding a breast in each hand. Earl walked over to me to adjust the cape, and wasn't looking at my breasts as he worked. I lifted each breast in sync with the words that came out of my mouth: "Hi, how are you!" I had turned my breasts into hand puppets! Earl fell apart laughing. He said, "It never fails. Women come in here all nervous and tense and by the third day, it's like this. But I've never seen this."

When the final day of shooting ended, I headed back home to wait for the article and the photos to arrive so I could give my approval, and the whole project would be finished. Or so I thought. No sooner did I arrive in Dallas, than Guccione's assistant called to say Bob wanted to personally take some photos. I really didn't want to. I didn't relish the thought of having to gear up emotionally again for a nude session, especially with Guccione as the photographer.

Every time I met with Bob Guccione, I was struck by his interesting look; it was disarming yet somehow appealing at the same time. His fashion sense is hopelessly stuck in the seventies. He has a deep tan and wears lots of gold chains with his shirt open halfway to his waist. He wears a hairpiece, and I'd swear he wears mascara, too, judging from how long and dark his eyelashes are. He just seemed so out-of-sync with the nineties. In spite of his out-of-date dress, he had a certain sexual appeal with his piercing blue eyes and obvious machismo. Let's face it, the man is a living legend.

He has a strong, almost overbearing personality. There is no question who is in control of his domain, his home, and his wife. Guccione's wife, Kathy Keaton, slithers around like a pussycat, claiming to be an independent woman, but there's no doubt she knows who's really the boss. He's also ruthless and can turn on you in a second.

Guccione knew my pictorial and article were going to be a hot ticket because of my connection with Bill Clinton, and because it would be a part of history, he just had to have his fingers in it. Even though it wasn't necessary for him to have much hands-on involvement with his empire, he liked to put his personal touch on certain projects. So I was summoned to New York, where he keeps a studio set up in his home. Although *Penthouse* has corporate offices in New York, Guccione works at home for the most part. He starts working at two in the afternoon and works through the night—like a vampire.

His home is one of the largest private residences in Manhattan. It's two brownstones combined and has five floors. He has an extensive and impressive art collection, including Picassos and Renoirs, and his furnishings have been imported from all over the world. For his personal safety and because of the value of his possessions, he keeps guards at the front. He also owns a gold-leaf piano that once belonged to Judy Garland, a magnificent piece. A lot of his furnishings are strange, though, with almost demonic overtones. I kept running into gargoyles and strange masks every time I turned a corner. And everything had an ancient smell to it.

The house had every luxury imaginable: an indoor swimming pool with Grecian statues peering out from every nook and cranny, a fully-equipped workout room, and guest rooms that are truly bizarre. On the occasions when I stayed there, they put me in a room that was decorated all in black, with mirrors on the ceiling. The bed had a canopy, and it was mirrored, too. It was stark black, with just little touches of red here and there. The Gucciones' thought it was an impressive piece of decorating, but it made me uncomfortable. It was confining and gave me a bad feeling.

An assistant, who worked with Roy True, came to New York with me once, and stayed in a room across the hall from my black room. She is a tall redhead with a strong personality. She wasn't one to be easily intimidated, but Guccione's house was enough to unsettle her. She tiptoed across the hall to my room the next morning and said she wouldn't stay in that house again, because it was so oppressive. Even worse, she couldn't sleep because she thought she could smell marijuana coming through the vents all night long, permeating her room. We found out later that Guccione's room was directly beneath hers.

The day of the photo shoot, I did my own makeup, and he worked without an assistant. He was trying so hard to be cool and sophisticated. This was the first time we had ever been alone together—his assistant was usually around, or I would have a representative with me. But that day it was just the two of us and his camera in the studio. He came in wearing his hairpiece and bedecked with enough gold chains to sink a ship. His denim shirt was unbuttoned almost to his navel, and I thought, "Doesn't anybody tell this guy people don't dress like that anymore?" It's a wonder he didn't fall over from the weight of all his chains.

He had his camera set up on a tripod, and as he was going back and forth, between the camera and me, he tripped over the tripod almost every time. I was trying hard not to laugh, because he was working so hard to be nonchalant, then he would trip over his tripod again and look very unsophisticated.

Whenever Earl Miller took a shot that showed my breasts, he asked me to make my nipples hard to make the photo look better. That was easy to do—I would just pinch them a little and they would stand right up. My session with Guccione was going fairly well until we came to a shot where my nipples had to be hard. He politely asked me to make them hard, but before I could respond, he asked, "Why don't I come over there with my tongue and help you out?"

This was exactly what I had anticipated I would be subjected to when the deal first came together, and I was pleasantly surprised when it didn't happen with Earl Miller. But now, here was the publisher himself, destroying my false sense of security by being offensive. I looked at him with his leering smile, and I have no doubt he would have been happy to oblige had I agreed. My temper flared, but I kept it in check so I could just get the session over with and get out of there. I brusquely replied, "No, thank you. I can do it." He got the message and didn't make any further offers.

The shots he took of me turned out quite good—pretty and soft. I knew he had a reputation as an accomplished photographer, and in the early days of the magazine did *everything* himself, including the photography.

I was anxious to escape Guccione's house as quickly as I could. Just walking into it made me feel trapped, like I might never get out again. That place gives off very bad psychic vibes. To my relief, the photo session ended and I threw my things together and left New York the same day.

The photo shoots and interviews with Art Harris all took place in the summer of 1992. According to my contract, Guccione had until the last day of fall to publish the article and pictorial, which gave him until late December. So it was completely up to him whether the magazine would hit the newsstands before or after the presidential election. I didn't really care when it came out. It was something I was doing to tell my story free of bias or spin and to set myself up financially—not to hurt Bill Clinton. If Guccione had an ulterior motive in deciding on the publication date, it made no difference to me.

I returned to New York again, to review the pictorial. I was pleased with it—the photos were extremely flattering. Now all that was left was to review and approve the article. Time kept dragging, though, and the article didn't come. Roy True called *Penthouse* a number of times asking when the article would be available for my review, and he was given lots of excuses and put off for one reason or another. I didn't like the warning signs I was getting about this article, but I tried to remain optimistic. I held fast to the belief that the final draft would appear in my mailbox any day, and I'd have the chance to repair any damage.

I couldn't have been more wrong.

Finis called me from Little Rock in mid-October. He had gotten yet another press release in his office, and told me I needed to see it. He faxed a copy to Roy True's office, and when I read it, I was stunned. It was from Guccione's office and said, in effect, he was releasing the magazine before the election to do damage control for Bill Clinton. The press release strongly suggested everything I alleged was probably untrue, and Guccione wanted to give Bill the opportunity to respond to my "sensational but unsubstantiated" charges before the election!

I knew I was in trouble. Was this Guccione's plan all along? Had his intent been only to discredit me instead of giving me the fair and unbiased treatment he had promised? It certainly seemed that way. I still hadn't seen the article, but the issue had already been printed. I had been set up and I went along willingly. Roy called Victor Kovner, Guccione's attorney, who was smooth as silk, apologetic but noncommittal.

Naturally, my first reaction was to sue Guccione's ass off. Although legal advisers assured me I had the basis for a lawsuit, they confirmed what I already suspected. Guccione has very deep pockets and is very patient. He could keep me tied up for years, financially and emotionally. I had already been used and abused so much, I just wasn't up to a protracted battle with someone who wouldn't hesitate to go for the jugular. I'm sure Guccione was betting that would be my reaction.

Besides, I still had the promise of back-end profits from the magazine—that was written into my contract. Guccione had reneged on my right to review the article to serve his own purpose, but I really didn't think he would cheat me financially. He might be able to sidestep the small points, but if he blatantly violated the financial terms of the contract, his credibility as a businessman would be destroyed.

Even though the magazine was available in some places by the middle of October, it officially went on sale the first week in November, right before the election, and copies were snatched up in record time. *Penthouse* had promised to give me a specified number of copies, but they never appeared. Finis bought an issue in Little

Rock, flew to Dallas with it that weekend, and that was the first time I saw it. I looked at the pictorial first and was thrilled. I was forty-two years old when those photos were taken, and I was proud of the way I looked. But then I read the article.

It would be easy to condemn Art Harris on the basis of what my friends and family told me about their interviews, but the truth is, I don't know how much of what he wrote was left out. He may have written my story from two different angles—pro-Gennifer and anti-Gennifer—but I'll never know. Jane Hamish, Guccione's assistant, told me Art turned in one hundred fifty pages of copy, but he had nothing to do with the final version, which was heavily edited. Guccione had the final say.

The article was definitely anti-Gennifer. Once again, I was portrayed as a gold-digging, no-talent, bleached-blonde bimbo. It was so hateful and mean that had it been about someone else, I would have had nothing but contempt for the shallow, greedy person Art Harris described. Bamboozled again. Why did I have to learn everything the hard way?

I tried to buy more copies of the magazine. As bad as the article was, since it was going to become a collector's item, I wanted to have a few on hand. (I understand that autographed copies have sold for as much as $2,000.) I certainly wasn't going to hold my breath and wait for *Penthouse* to come through with the copies they had promised me. I went from newsstand to newsstand looking for it and was told the same thing everywhere I went: Merchants had received only a limited number of copies, and they sold out quickly.

I found this curious. Why were so few copies being distributed when the issue was such a hot seller? I called various distributors around the country, posing as someone interested in getting a shipment of the magazine, and was told by most of them that they would love to have gotten more copies, but they had been told they probably wouldn't. It seemed that *Penthouse* had distributed far fewer than they normally did. It wasn't a matter of the magazines jumping off the shelves so fast they couldn't keep them stocked, there just weren't many available.

I thought back to a conversation I had had with Guccione during which he said he was concerned about the possibility of a conservative justice being appointed to the Supreme Court. Magazines such as *Penthouse* were constantly being sued under obscenity laws, and all Guccione needed was a conservative majority on the Supreme Court to start losing some of those lawsuits.

He wanted Bill Clinton, a liberal, to win the presidential election. Then when there was a vacancy on the Supreme Court, Bill would appoint a liberal justice to fill it. I began to wonder if I was nothing more than a pawn in his efforts to help get Bill elected. It seemed he made me look as bad as he possibly could have in order to discredit me and win support for Bill. That must be why Guccione was so eager to secure my story. It wasn't about money, it was about damage control for Bill. His negative portrayal of me helped to secure his own future by helping to elect a Democrat. He avoided the risk of *Playboy* presenting my story honestly, which might have hurt Bill's chances.

I never received a dime beyond the initial advance. The advance was generous, yes, but it certainly didn't give me long-term financial security. Furthermore, Guccione owns the rights to all the photos taken of me, and if he ever felt he could make money by using them, he wouldn't be obligated to pay me even a nickel. He knew what he was doing all along and knew he could get away with it, too.

Meanwhile, I had my mother to consider. She knew about the deal from the beginning, but I knew she wouldn't ever be fully prepared to see her daughter in *Penthouse*, in the flesh, so to speak. We had talked about it at length, and she was supportive but apprehensive. I was talking to her on the telephone shortly after the magazine came out, and while we were talking, my stepfather came home with a copy. I hadn't planned on that. I wanted Mother to see it and have a chance to digest it, then we would talk about it.

I had promised Mother I wouldn't show "the precious." I made a solemn vow there would be no spread-eagle shots, nothing lewd or vulgar. Even though I make my own decisions regardless of Mother's opinion, she has a large influence in my life and I have always at least listened to her. And I agreed with her on that point.

Anyway, Jim came in and handed her the *Penthouse* while we were talking. I gulped, and thought "Oh, no, I don't want sit here on the phone with her while she goes through it page by page." But I couldn't just hang up on her. She started looking at it right away. "Oh, Sissy, this cover is so pretty. You look so pretty." Mother had a poodle for years that she jokingly referred to as my brother. Hence, the nickname Sissy.

She started turning the pages and was happily exclaiming,

"Those are pretty shots of you." She turned to the next page and her praise lost some of its exuberance. "Well, your little bottom sure is cute," she said reluctantly. I was dying inside. She turned another page and the tone of her voice changed dramatically. "Oh. You told me you weren't going to show the precious." "Now, Mother," I hastily replied, "I didn't spread my legs." "Well, close enough," she shot back.

Actually, she took it pretty well. She hated the article—absolutely hated it—but with the exception of the one picture that showed my precious, she handled it very well. I didn't want my stepfather to see it, though. I begged Mother, "Don't let Pop see the pictures." I could deal with Mother, but there was something about having my stepfather see a nude layout of me that I just couldn't cope with. I'm sure he must have seen the pictures eventually, but, bless him, he never let on if he did.

Finis was extremely displeased with the article, too. We had been in touch frequently over the past several months, and he was anticipating a fair treatment in the story, just as I was. Anyone who knew me at all thought it was a real bad piece. It painted such a dreadful picture of me living in splendor off the proceeds of all the men I had taken money from. The description of my apartment made it sound like a "love palace." I wished I lived in the place described in the article!

Finis did like the pictorial, though. It was hard not to like. For all Guccione's underhandedness, he did make me look beautiful visually. Fortunately, Finis is open-minded and also appreciates the value of a good deal, which we initially thought it was.

Unlike Guccione, I felt honor bound to fulfill my contractual obligations, which meant returning to New York to promote the magazine. I told Jane Hamish I had no intention of staying in Guccione's house, however. I was so angry with him anyway, and I didn't want to stay in that black room again. Jane called me back and told me Guccione was very hurt. At least he pretended to be. Against my better judgment, she talked me into staying there because the few promotional events they had set up were scheduled with the assumption I would be staying at the house.

As much as I dreaded going back to Guccione's house, I was hoping it would give me the opportunity to talk with him face to face. I'd had no luck reaching him by telephone—my calls were never put through once the magazine came out. And he refused to return my calls. Even though I was staying in his house, I never could nail him down. He managed to successfully avoid me and the confrontation I wanted to have with him.

Before I left Dallas for New York, I did an interview with one of the local TV stations. That station carried *Inside Edition*, and, coincidentally, a representative from *Inside Edition* was in Dallas when I did the interview. Without my knowledge or permission, he used my interview on his own program. When I got to New York I was scheduled to do an interview with *A Current Affair*, and when their people saw me on *Inside Edition*, they were furious.

We went ahead with the interview anyway, but Mary Garafolla, the interviewer, was mad before we even started because she had lost her exclusivity. It was one of the most mean-spirited grillings I had ever gotten. She started off by telling me she thought it was vulgar for Bill and me to have pet names for our private body parts. As if I cared what her opinion was.

But I tried to help her relate. I asked her if she had a boyfriend, although I doubted it with the thighs she was carrying around. But she surprised me by saying yes. So I asked her, "Don't you call each other by affectionate little names?" She just answered with a short, snotty "No." I'm sure if her boyfriend had any pet names for her, they weren't the kind he could say to her face.

Besides *A Current Affair*, I did a few radio shows and newspaper interviews, and had been scheduled to appear on the *Phil Donahue Show*, but out of the blue, Phil refused to have me on his show. I was immediately suspicious because I thought maybe *Penthouse* had a hand in it, trying to limit the magazine's promotion as well as it's distribution. I had Roy True call the *Phil Donahue Show* to find out exactly why they didn't want me on the show then, when a few months earlier they had practically knocked down my door trying to get me to appear. The reason they gave Roy was they changed their mind because I admitted having had an abortion. Mr. Liberal, Phil Donahue, wouldn't allow me on his show because I had had an abortion. Go figure.

The whole *Penthouse* experience was a hard-learned lesson in the ongoing education of Gennifer Flowers. I knew I didn't have the ability to deal with people like Bob Guccione and his lawyer on my own, but I believed if I surrounded myself with good advisers, people who were experts in their field, I would be covered. I found out otherwise. There just wasn't any way to anticipate the extent to which people would take advantage of me, and once I found out, it was too late. The fact was, Guccione's attorney, Victor Kovner, had simply "out-lawyered" Roy True.

Kovner himself might have had something at stake, since he is well connected with the Democratic Party.

But my philosophy is the same as it always has been: learn from it and move on. Just don't ever let it happen again. Unfortunately, every situation is different. I couldn't possibly anticipate every bump in the road, and there still were some unhappy surprises in store for me.

Thirteen

The whole *Penthouse* experience left me feeling frustrated and vulnerable. I didn't trust anyone, and I became so protective of myself that it was all I could do to survive day by day. Consequently, I became unable to open myself intimately to anyone. For over a year, I became celibate. I felt used and abused by men. The man I had loved for 12 years had turned his back on me. Then Art Harris and Bob Guccione had wooed me over only to fry me over the coals. I just didn't want to put myself anywhere near a situation where I could be hurt and used again.

At first it was hard going without sex because I'm a sexual person. I had to get over the physical desire for intimacy; then I had to overcome the loneliness that a lack of intimacy with anyone can bring. Eventually, I became quite comfortable and almost preferred it that way. It wasn't until Finis and I decided to try to rekindle our romance that I gave up my celibacy. That too was difficult. But Finis is a patient, loving man and he helped through the emotional aspects of the transition.

On the positive side, my *Penthouse* appearance generated lots of interest by various media sources throughout the United States and Europe. Requests for appearances and interviews came in on a regular basis, and I decided to take advantage of some of them. I had still never had the chance to present my side of the story. So I decided to maintain a high profile until I could figure out the best way to convince the public I was telling the truth—I *did* have an affair with Bill Clinton, but the facts had been twisted and manipulated to the point where people were doubtful it had ever happened.

I admit there were some elements of my notoriety I was enjoying. I've always liked being the center of attention, and there were times when the attention wasn't all bad. Some of the opportunities I was offered were just plain fun, and I agreed to do them as a way of easing the tension and pressure I was constantly feeling. One of the most irresistible offers came from the HBO show *Dream On* asking if

I would consider a guest appearance. I was to play a news reporter, and that appealed to me immensely. It would be pleasant to be on the other side for a change!

The show was shot in Los Angeles, and the studio was in a big, metal barn-like structure. I was nervous about doing this, although my part wasn't large, and the filming wouldn't take long, I wasn't used to acting. I did have my experience at KARK to draw on, however.

Blake Hendrix came with me—more out of curiosity than to serve as my attorney. We got to watch several scenes being shot before my scene came up.

I was on the set, in costume and made up, and I had yet to see the script. All of a sudden, the director yelled, "Action!" I kind of held my hand up and said, "Excuse me, I don't know what my lines are." The staff had completely forgotten to get the script to me!

The director rolled his eyes, and I felt like dropping through the floor. Fortunately, I had only a few lines, and I memorized them quickly. The acting part wasn't hard at all. I just drew on my memories of what it had been like when I worked for the TV station, and it was like being on the job again.

Seeing everything that went on behind the scenes was the best part of it. Two other cameo guests were on the show, as well: Rita Jenrette, whose former husband was a congressman who had been convicted on federal bribery charges; and Jessica Hahn, who gained notoriety as a result of her affair with Jim Bakker, the televangelist. Actress Terri Garr played a politician's wife who had an affair with Brian Benben, the show's star. George Hamilton played the politician—and he was gorgeous.

The show ran during a ratings sweep and I was flattered that they used my name in the promotional spots for the program. I did this show just for the fun of it, since I certainly wasn't going to get rich on the $700 they paid me. But I did get interviewed by *Entertainment Tonight*.

Brian Benben was adorable, and I enjoyed watching him do his scenes. It seemed to me he was overacting at the time, and I thought it would turn out corny. But when I saw the tape, it was perfect. He obviously knew what he was doing.

Rita, Jessica, and I had each done our scenes separately, so we hadn't met until we got together to do some promotional shots for the show. Rita was very cool and reserved, but a nice lady. We were waiting for Jessica to show up, and she was late. All of a sudden I heard a commotion in the hall. It was Jessica, coming down the hall, yelling "Gennifer, Gennifer, Gennifer." She barreled into the room and came up about two inches from my face and said, "Oh, Gennifer, I have wanted to meet you so badly, and I want you to know I understand what you're going through, and you can count on me."

Then she jokingly said, "If you fix me up with Bill Clinton, I'll fix you up with Jim Bakker." I was having trouble seeing the humor in her suggestion. Jim Bakker was certainly not my idea of a sexually attractive man. I couldn't resist. I took her aside and very quietly told her, "No offense, Jessica, but I wouldn't fuck him on a bad day." She laughed and whispered, "I don't blame you."

We did the photo shoot, with Rita and I dressed rather conservatively, and Jessica with her little bitty black skirt and mesh top that was distinctly see-through. She was very attractive and had gone to great lengths to appear sexy, but she took herself a little too seriously for my taste.

Part of my obligation to promote *Penthouse* was a scheduled appearance on the Howard Stern radio show. I dreaded meeting Howard because he had such a bigger-than-life reputation, and heaven only knew what he would do with me. I had heard his show for the first time when I was in Los Angeles, doing the *Penthouse* shoot, and I was infuriated by some of the things he said. He was so abrasive that I actually got fighting mad just listening to him . . . a reaction he's known for encouraging.

Then it hit me what a showman he really is. He was saying things that many people think, but don't have the guts to say. I'm not convinced Howard believes everything he says, but he sure knows how to get a reaction from his listeners.

I arrived at the studio very early in the morning—five-thirty or six—and walked into the control room expecting to see a green-eyed, fire-breathing dragon. But the first thing I noticed was his beautiful head of hair. Then he turned around and gave me a puppy-dog look that melted my heart on the spot. He was a true stud-muffin!

Howard was very kind to me. He didn't pull too many punches in his interview, but he treated me fairly. We liked each other right away, and I have to admit I have a real crush on him. The man has an energy about him and is incredibly sexy.

I appeared on his show one more time, after I made the tapes of my telephone conversations with Bill available to the public. He subsequently asked me to join him to help celebrate the addition of another station to the ones already broadcasting his show. I wasn't able to do that, but I would have liked to. I enjoyed being around him and was glad that I had guessed right: his abrasive personality was all for show.

I must have done dozens of remote radio interviews sitting on the floor of my kitchen, talking on the telephone, one show after another with no break in between. During one interview, I had to go to the bathroom so bad I couldn't wait. But the show was only half finished, and I could hardly excuse myself right in the middle of it to go use the potty. Desperate for relief, I looked around the kitchen and got the brilliant idea to use a bowl. So as I continued to answer questions about Bill Clinton and me, I proceeded to tinkle into the bowl. Luckily it wasn't stainless steel, so it didn't make any noise. If the listeners only knew what was going on while they were asking me all those serious questions! But when nature calls . . . .

My first offer to make an appearance in a foreign country came from a television show in Spain, the *De Tu A Tu* show. The show is similar to *The Tonight Show* in the United States, but it's the only one in Spain—no competition. Plus, it's seen in other countries around Europe, too. Spanish culture is nighttime oriented, and the show's viewership was enormous. The producer sent me first class tickets to Madrid and paid me a substantial amount of money for the appearance.

When I agreed to go to Spain, Finis came with me. He and I had never completely lost touch with each other. Even though our romantic relationship had fizzled, he had been a constant source of support for me, for which I was grateful. Gradually we started seeing each other again and had started rebuilding what we once had shared.

We were treated like royalty by the flight attendants on our first-class flight over. In fact, we received first-class treatment throughout our stay in Spain. It was a long flight, and I was anxious to get to the hotel and unpack. Before we landed, I brushed my teeth and combed my hair, but didn't bother re-doing my makeup because I didn't expect anyone but a representative from the show to be waiting to meet us. We gathered our luggage and made it through customs. As we exited the secured area into the airport terminal, I was horrified to see more than two dozen reporters and cameramen swarming toward us snapping pictures and asking for interviews.

I was totally unprepared for the press—I looked a wreck! I grabbed my sunglasses, shoved them on, and smiled wide—at least my teeth were brushed. I was flattered by the press attention and their excitement that Gennifer with a "G" had arrived.

The representatives from the show were there to meet us and were concerned that someone might corner me and infringe on their exclusivity. So they stood close by and let me do just a short interview with the gathered press.

Europeans, I quickly learned, associated my relationship with Bill with that of John Kennedy and Marilyn Monroe. We saw that printed in several publications. Everyone thought our whole affair was as romantic as could be, and they wanted to hear all about it. But as much as they loved hearing about the romance, they were even more interested in the political aspects of the story. They knew that Bill, as president of the most powerful country in the world, could have an effect on economies around the world. Because of that, his actions could affect their lives, so they wanted to know more about this man.

From the airport we were taken to the beautiful Palace Hotel, and it was crawling with more members of the media. But they were courteous and non-intrusive. Europeans are more liberal in their opinions about extramarital affairs, so no one subjected me to harsh or judgmental questioning the entire time I was there. What a pleasant change.

The television studio was out of town and I was amazed when we got there at how modern and well-equipped the dressing rooms and makeup area were. We were shown into the manager's office and saw photos of previous guests on show. I specifically remember a picture of Michael Jackson. (Not bad company to be in.) During the rehearsal of a song I was planning to sing on the show, Finis noticed everyone was smiling. He asked the director why and was told that they were surprised and impressed with my voice. Since all of this has happened, my singing has had to take a back seat. So it was nice to hear someone say that again.

When we talked to the show's producers before making the trip over, they told me they planned to pay me in *cash*, American dollars. That made me real nervous. This was my first trip overseas and I didn't know if I was being set up or what. I was still concerned that my Bill Clinton connection might cause someone to do something to hurt me, and I had heard stories about drugs being planted in people's luggage when they were in foreign countries. I didn't want to end up in jail.

The stories I mentioned earlier about how people who had crossed Bill ended up seriously injured were still fresh in my mind, too. Even more disturbing than those accounts, though, was an incident that took place shortly after Bill was elected.

Jerry Parks, who was head of the Little Rock presidential campaign headquarters during the early days of the campaign, was reportedly writing a book about Bill and Arkansas politics. He was murdered, shot several times as he was driving his car, and all his notes and tapes vanished, never to surface again. Needless to say, I was more than a little concerned for my own safety.

Finis and I went to the studio to do the show, and, sure enough, they paid me in cash—several thousand dollars in stacks of hundred dollar bills. I counted them out right there in the dressing room. Thank goodness Finis was with me; he agreed to hold the money while I did the show. I couldn't imagine being on stage with hundred dollar bills stuffed in my pockets. I would have been unable to concentrate.

On the show with me that evening were the rock band INXS; Spain's premier bull fighter, who was retiring; and Franco's grandson.

The show was over, it was one o'clock in the morning, and somehow Finis and I had to get back to our hotel with all that cash. I was so nervous about it I was shaking. I felt we had to come up with a plan. Finis had a colleague in Madrid, Allister Seymour, whom he had called as soon as we arrived in Spain. Allister came to the show, and afterward we asked him if he would take us back to the hotel. The show had provided a chauffeured limousine for us, but I wasn't about to get into a car with a strange driver and take my chances.

We didn't tell the driver we weren't going with him until the last minute. Finis told him we had made other arrangements, we jumped into Allister's car, and sped to the hotel at over a hundred miles per hour. Allister knew I was scared and anxious to get to the hotel. We screeched to a stop in front of the hotel, ran into the lobby and handed the money to the desk clerk to lock up in the hotel's safe. I knew there were no guarantees it would stay there, but I felt much better not having all that cash on me.

As a result of the exposure I got on the television show, everywhere I turned the next day, there were press people waiting hopefully for an interview! I literally could not walk down the street without being mobbed. Every two feet someone would stop me and ask for my autograph, and the press tailed me in droves. I finally had to arrange a hasty series of interviews because the hotel had become a zoo with all the reporters milling around. I gave five hours of unplanned interviews that day! This was the first time I didn't feel threatened by the media. The Spanish press was refreshing and I felt comfortable enough with them to have Finis take a picture of me standing in the middle of a group of them. If I did that at home, I'd likely walk away with a knife in my back.

The rest of the trip was a delight. Allister took us to see authentic Flamenco dancers, we dined in wonderful restaurants, and I danced the night away in a disco with Spain's Prince Felipe. When it was time to return home, though, I had to deal with my fear of customs finding something that had been planted in one of my bags. I inspected everything thoroughly when I packed, but I couldn't quell the butterflies I had when we approached customs in the United States. The drug-sniffing dogs were waiting, and I could envision them finding something I didn't know about, and I'd be a dead duck. I held my breath as I moved past the area where the dogs were on duty, and exhaled in relief when they didn't even twitch. The custom's agent inspected my suitcase with only mild interest and waved me on, thank goodness. I made it through safely without any unpleasant surprises, but I really resented having to worry about being set up.

A year or so after my trip to Spain, *The Thomas Gotschick Show*, a German version of *The Tonight Show*, invited me to come to Germany and appear on the show. They, too, offered me a fee to appear, and provided first class travel and treatment. Every once in awhile there are some benefits to this ordeal! I took my mother with me this time, which brought a fresh wave of anxiety. I prayed the trip would go smoothly because she was with me, and I dreaded the thought of anything ugly or unpleasant happening.

Of all the changes I have experienced in my life since the *Star* story broke in 1992, the worst is that I continue to fear for my life. That fear has not abated, and I still take extraordinary measures to ensure my security. I live in a tightly secured apartment building with guards in the lobby and hardly ever travel alone. When I go out alone, I try to go unnoticed, usually wearing a baseball cap pulled down over my hair. I live in semi-seclusion, and it is not a pleasant way to live.

So it was with some apprehension that I left for Germany with Mother. She had never been to Europe before, and I desperately wanted the trip to go well. We arrived in Munich and were met by a representative from the show driving a fabulous Mercedes limousine. He greeted us enthusiastically and drove us to the luxurious hotel where we were staying. The hotel was beautiful and elegant and located in a part of Munich that was much like Rodeo Drive in Beverly Hills. The whole city was clean, pristine and safe . . . most refreshing. We were told that a woman could go out alone at two in the morning without fear of being raped. They told us rape is almost nonexistent there. It was also exciting to be surrounded by all that beautiful architecture, not to mention the rich history of the city.

The next day, the producer of the show personally came to the hotel to pick us up. He graciously told me how important my appearance was to him and that I would have top billing over Steven Seagal, the actor; Rue McClanahan, from the *Golden Girls* television show; and an Olympic skier who had just won his second gold medal. Wow, what a guest list! We had a leisurely conversation with him, then departed for the show. On the way to the studio, the producer got a worried look on his face, then frantically reached for the car phone. They had forgotten to send a car for Rue McClanahan, and she had to take a taxi!

Mother and I were shown into a dressing room, and as I got ready, we talked eagerly of meeting Rue McClanahan. We both were fans of *The Golden Girls* and got the biggest kick out of having the chance to meet her so far from home. When I was ready, I left Mother and went to the make-up room. Rue was there already, and I couldn't wait to introduce myself and tell her how eager Mother was to meet her, too. We made eye contact for just an instant, then she cut her eyes away without saying a word.

This snub from her just didn't make sense. I thought I was imagining things and kept waiting for her to turn around and acknowledge my presence. I was standing four feet away from her, and she pretended I didn't exist. I certainly wasn't going to force myself on her, so when it became obvious she would rather have been dipped in hot tar than say hello to me, I went to my corner of the makeup room. I sure didn't want the same thing to happen to Mother.

I went back to where Mother was waiting, and the first thing she asked me was if I had met Rue. I told her, "Yes, but just briefly." I didn't want to tell her what really happened. It was important to me that *nothing* spoil the trip for her. But it was obvious Rue had a problem with me.

Mother was seated in the front row, and just as the show was starting, the band played and Thomas Gotschick collected Mother out of the audience and danced her around the stage. She was absolutely sparkling with pleasure, and I was relieved and happy she was having a good time.

The set of the show was elaborate, with beautiful colors and comfortable furniture. It was structured so that there was a steep stairway that came down through the audience. The featured guest would descend the stairs while the other guests would enter from side doors at floor level. I was the featured guest, and as the show began, I found myself at the top of the staircase. All the lights and cameras were on me, the song "Isn't She Lovely" was playing in the background, and all I could see was what seemed like a thousand steps I had to make my way down without falling. That was no easy feat in four-inch heels. I mentally crossed my fingers, smiled wide, took a deep breath, and plunged ahead. All the way down I silently thanked Mother for sending me to charm school so I knew how to walk down stairs.

I reached the stage without mishap, and a little microphone was placed in my ear to translate Thomas Gotschick's questions. He would ask me questions in German, they would be translated for me, I would respond in English, and my answer would be translated back to German for the audience. It was tricky making the procedure seem smooth, but they pulled it off easily.

Thomas Gotschick was a gorgeous and charming man who spoke impeccable English. He was easy to talk with and seemed excited to have me on the show. We chatted awhile, then it was time for the other guests to appear. Out of one of the side doors came the Olympic skier, then Rue, and finally Steven Seagal, who was just a big ol' hunk of burnin' love sitting there. My heart was doing flip-flops just looking at that gorgeous man. Unlike Rue, he was *very* glad to meet me. We spent some time together talking after the show, and sparks started flying.

He and I were talking, the electricity coursing back and forth between us, and Mother kept interrupting. I put her off saying, "I'll be finished in just a minute, Mother," but she wasn't having any part of it. She marched right up to us and said, "Gennifer, he's married. We don't want to go through that again." I was speechless for a moment, then Steven and I both burst out laughing. "You've got a point there," I agreed. Thanks to Mother, that was the end of *that* conversation!

Backstage was a wall where all the guests from the show would sign their autograph. I didn't realize Rue was standing right behind me while I was autographing the wall, and when I finished, I stepped back and practically landed on top of her. I turned to her and said, "I'm so sorry. Please, excuse me." Rue wouldn't say a word. It seemed that I could have put my spike heel through her foot and she still wouldn't have reacted.

Aside from McClanahan's cold-shoulder treatment, the trip was a success. I was treated so differently on European talk shows than I was on U.S. talk shows; it was truly a pleasure. These people were interested in hearing what I had to say, not in what *they* wanted me to say as was so often the case in the United States. I never minded tough questions—in fact, I expected them—but I was disturbed by how American interviewers would try to manipulate my answers for their own purposes.

Virtually every television talk show host in the United States asked me to appear at one time or another, including Geraldo, Montel Williams, Jenny Jones, and, of course, Phil Donahue until he found out I'd had an abortion. I agreed to do only a few: the *Bertice Berry Show*, and the *Leeza Show* among them. I did those shows because the timing seemed right and they sounded like fun.

I have given interviews for a multitude of magazines and newspapers around the world. In some cases the interviews were okay, but, more often than not, I found my words had been twisted to put me in a bad light. I'll never forget the first time I read an article from one of those interviews. I was dumbfounded at some of the fabricated quotes attributed to me, and was even more astonished at how things I actually did say were put in a different context that made me sound awful. It's unbelievably frustrating to read an article after an interview, only to think, "Wait! I didn't say that!" or "That's not what I meant!"

What continues to astonish me is that whenever magazines or newspapers interview me, they demand substantiation for my claims, which I happily give them. They press me unmercifully, trying to find something to trip me up that might invalidate my story. But then they turn to other sources, to people who claim to know me, who make outrageously untruthful statements, and those statements are accepted as fact and are printed.

A lot of people knew about my relationship with Bill Clinton, and some have given their opinions to the public through the media, some good some bad. As long as they told the truth, I didn't care. What infuriates me is all the people who have come out of the woodwork claiming to be my "best friend" or former "roommate" and proceed to try to discredit me.

If I gathered all the people who swear they were my best friend or roommate, Yankee Stadium would be too small to hold them all. Yet so-called investigative reporters will print wild accusations as if they were the gospel truth without so much as doing a background check on these people to see if they even knew me! A tiny bit of investigating would reveal most of these people as frauds.

The media has a lot of nerve questioning my honesty and integrity when they sacrifice truth for the sake of a good story and ratings. And they call *me* a bimbo! The attitude seems to be, why mess up a good story with the facts? There was a time when I thought the media would be my salvation. Well, my bubble has sure been popped. The fact is, the American public is being misled on a daily basis by the so-called mainstream media.

Take Rush Limbaugh, for example. I'm well aware that his shows are designed to entertain as well as inform, but I really thought he was more concerned with honesty and spreading the truth for the sake of the country. I did a phone interview with Rush at his request, although he is fond of saying *I* called *him* to initiate the interview, which is absolutely untrue. For the most part, it was an amiable conversation, and I was grateful to him for emphatically affirming that I was the only woman who had proof of what I was claiming.

During the course of the conversation, something was said about *Penthouse*. I made the comment that I was disappointed in the article, and Rush responded, "Oh, come on, Gennifer, you're a big girl. You should know what to expect." I replied that big girl or not, I expected people to do what they told me they were going to do, to be honorable and abide by their agreements.

What I didn't know was the interview was being taped for later broadcast, and Rush cut the tape off right after he said, "You should know what to expect." I heard the broadcast later that day, and my response to him had disappeared. He continued, saying if Guccione had taken me, it was my own fault. No one ever heard the rest of the conversation.

All the audience heard was Rush's final word!

Fourteen

From the moment I mentioned in the *Star* article that I had tapes of my phone conversations with Bill Clinton, I have been pressured to make them available to the public. I didn't think the excerpts printed by the *Star* presented the whole picture, so I was anxious to release them, too. My one attempt to do so, during the campaign, had stirred up so much trouble I thought it best to back off for awhile. But I was finally convinced the time was right. I had the tapes reproduced and wrote a booklet containing an explanation of what was going on when the conversations took place. I also included a full written transcript of what was said. I had forensic experts verify that the voices on the tapes were Bill's and mine and that the tapes had never been altered.

My motive for releasing the tapes was not to get rich from the proceeds of the sales, but to put the truth out to the American people, and to let them hear Bill in his own words prove he is willing to manipulate and lie. The tapes are the *only* real proof of that, so far.

The tapes and booklet were released under the title *Setting the Record Straight,* and I hoped to be able to do just that by making the tapes available via an 800 number on television and radio. Plus, I had been through so many interviews and shows in the previous two years, I felt there were certain people I could depend on to help get the message out.

Rush Limbaugh was one of those people. I believed he truly understood the importance of letting the American people see exactly what kind of president was running their country. He said so often enough on his show. But to my surprise, Rush personally turned down my advertisement. He wouldn't allow it on either his radio or his television show and would never say why.

I was crushed and confused. I thought he would jump at the opportunity to offer proof of all the things he had been saying about Bill: that Bill was a smooth manipulator, that he tried to cover up the truth, and that he and I *did* have an affair. Rush had built a career around these allegations, and yet he wouldn't accept the opportunity to offer definitive proof—in Bill's own words. The only thing I could speculate was that Rush wants to bat Bill around like a ball of yarn, but he doesn't want to knock him down completely. Bill Clinton is a cash cow for Rush Limbaugh, and he wants to stretch his Clinton-bashing routine out as long as possible.

All three major networks turned me down, as did The Fox Network and Turner Broadcasting. No one would touch my ad. That wasn't as surprising as Rush's refusal, but it did put me in a quandary. My marketing would have to be extremely inventive if anyone was to learn the tapes were available. My agent arranged a press conference, and to my gratification, it got a lot of attention. CNN carried it live, and most major newspapers and radio and television stations covered it.

Then I began accepting appearances on talk shows again, both radio and television. Howard Stern had me on again, as did Barry Farber, who has a show in New York City similar to Rush Limbaugh's. Barry is a man who has tremendous respect for his country, and he was absolutely fair and objective. He wasn't on my side, he wasn't on Bill's side. He just tried to cover the story from all angles.

Then came Rolonda. The executive producer of the *Rolonda* show had spoken with my business manager and asked if I would appear on her show. Not having much luck in getting television exposure for the tapes, I thought this would be an excellent opportunity. I was assured both verbally and in writing that the program would be objective, that Rolonda would not attack me or be combative, and that I would be the only one on the stage. I was eager to get an appropriate forum.

The producer wanted to bring in, by remote camera, the state troopers who had worked for Bill, and that was fine with me. They had recently started telling their stories about Bill's sexual escapades while governor of Arkansas, and they were also willing to corroborate my story.

The morning of the show, a limousine picked up my manager and me to take us to the studio. The building was rather nondescript, and once we got inside it didn't improve a whole lot. To get inside, we had to be escorted past a line of people waiting to get in to see the show. Most of the furniture was vintage '60s, not real impressive. There was a platter of cheese and fruit—standard fare in talk show green rooms.

The executive producer came in to greet us and couldn't have been nicer. He graciously welcomed us to the show, all the while knowing he was about to throw me to the lions.

Waiting in the green room for the show to start, I expected Rolonda to stop by to introduce herself and say hello. I had done enough of these shows by then to know the procedure—the host always made a point of popping in even if just for a minute before going on stage. Rolonda never showed. I was a little suspicious, but went onstage when it was time.

I was seated in plenty of time to scan the audience, which I always do for a number of reasons. For one thing, I check to make sure there are no crazies there who might have sneaked an gun into the studio to shoot me. I also like to get a feel for the audience . . . how are they dressed, do they look educated and classy, or do they look like a bunch of ingrates who are eager to take out their frustrations on me just because I exist? Rolonda's audience definitely fell into the later category, with a few exceptions.

Rolonda became combative almost immediately. She would ask me a question and before I got more than three or four words out of my mouth, she would interrupt with another question, or exclaim, "Oh Gennifer, that's not true." She would turn her back on me while I was in mid-sentence and rile the audience up with looks of incredulity or sounds of disbelief. The audience responded by hooting and hollering, and it was rapidly turning into a sideshow.

Members of the audience had a chance to ask me questions, but it was engineered so they never really asked me anything—they just vented their smug disapproval, egged on by Rolonda. One or two audience members tried to speak out on my behalf, and she shut them down quickly and moved on to someone who was willing to sling mud at me. The more sensational and ugly it became, the more Rolonda liked it. Ratings! Once again, objectivity and fairness were tossed out the window for the sake of ratings.

My blood was starting to boil. I was so weary of being blind-sided time after time, and it was happening again. But I deliberately kept my cool, maintaining a benign expression and trying to hold my own without letting it appear she was getting to me. I'm sure she would have loved it had I stormed off the stage, but I wasn't about to give her the satisfaction.

The state troopers were brought in by remote, and Rolonda started in on them. One of the troopers, Roger Perry, told her flat out that he and Bill Clinton had once had a conversation about their troubled marriages, and Bill admitted to him he was in love with another woman. Roger said he just naturally assumed that woman was me. He had known about me for a long time—as had most of the other troopers who worked for Bill. That shut Rolonda up for a second, but it didn't take her long to get nasty again.

The troopers were sitting in a studio in another town and were being brought into Rolonda's studio on a big screen. We could see them, but they couldn't see us. During the break, Rolonda started to make fun of the troopers and the expressions on their faces as they sat waiting to be interviewed. She got the audience laughing at them, too. It was very inappropriate, not to mention unprofessional.

At one point during the show, three journalists were brought onstage and seated beside me, in direct violation of our contract. I was shocked and wondered why they were there. I knew it wouldn't be to my benefit. It turned out that two of them had been told to take Bill Clinton's side, and one was supposed to support me. The journalist on my side, Andrew Ferguson of the *New York Times*, was given about fifteen seconds to make his case, and was able to make an excellent point. He said maybe people should quit trying to examine my motives and listen carefully to the tapes because they really weren't flattering to Clinton.

The other two mostly offered criticism of me, but neither of them really had anything of substance to say, it was all for show. Especially when one of the journalists, Jane Furse of the *New York Daily News*, was talking about Paula Jones' sexual harassment suit and made what she thought was a clever wisecrack. She said anybody who believed Paula's encounter with Bill Clinton was sexual harassment probably believed I was a natural blonde. I was furious, and I shook my head in disbelief. What an unprofessional witch!

The show was nearly over, thank goodness, because I was ready to explode. As soon as I was sure the cameras were off and the microphones were no longer live, I leaned across Andy Ferguson, nudged him back, and shook my finger at Jane Furse. "You listen up,"

I told her, angrily. "You ever take a cheap shot like that at me again and I'll knock your skinny ass out of that chair so fast you won't know what hit you."

Jane didn't say anything, she just kind of blinked in surprise. But I was wound up by then, and I kept going. "I have never claimed to be a natural blonde," I continued. "But if you want to talk about what's real, my tits are real." All three of them sat there stunned and speechless. I tore off my microphone, stood up, thanked Andy Ferguson for attempting to support me, and was out of there. I couldn't believe it. As the limo pulled away from the studio headed back to the hotel, I broke down, sobbing uncontrollably as my whole body shook with tension. How could Rolonda and that bunch of idiots she works for live with themselves? They were brutal.

The past few years have taught me a lot. I've learned whom I can trust and whom I cannot. And there are about half a dozen people in the first category—I call those "the precious few." Most startling to me has been learning how deceptive the American press is. The American people depend on the media to give them facts and objective analysis, and the majority of what is being fed to the public is filled with inaccuracies, private agendas, and personal opinion. When it comes to reporting stories like mine and those of the troopers that cast doubt on Bill Clinton's character, the mainstream media in this country has shown supreme arrogance.

Two highly respected reporters from the *Los Angeles Times* learned this. Bill Remple and Doug Frantz began covering Bill Clinton before the presidential election. They were the ones who originally reported the draft-dodging allegations against him. And they were looking into Whitewater long before others jumped on the bandwagon. The spent many months in Little Rock, digging for information. There goal was never to hurt Bill; they were just following up on the leads that came their way.

They had planned to break the Troopergate story, too. They were the first reporters to interview the troopers who ultimately came forward. They later told us they had the story all wrapped up and ready to go, but when they submitted it, their editors chose to sit on it until after the *American Spectator*, a conservative monthly magazine, broke the story. Bill and Doug knew they had the same story. In fact, they had gotten to the troopers before the other publication. The editors at the *Times*, however, chose to minimize any problems with the White House by letting the other publication run with the story.

Bill and Doug were so upset and frustrated by this gutlessness. Doug actually quit the *Times* and went to work at the *New York Times* as a financial writer, swearing to never again report on politics.

Another encounter with the mainstream media only confirmed my feelings about their lack of responsibility. When I was preparing to release the tapes, I got a call from Marilyn Thompson, a highly respected editor with the *Washington Post*. She pleaded with me to be able to come to Dallas and just listen to the tapes. She agreed to sign a document promising not to print anything about them without my written consent. At the last minute, she was unable to make it and another reporter was sent. This woman came to my house and listened to all the tapes. Afterward she told me, "Gennifer, I've got to tell you. After listening to all these tapes, if there was ever any doubt in my mind about your story and your relationship with Bill Clinton, its completely gone now." She knew we had a story and she promised to get back to me in a few days.

When I didn't hear from her, I had my agent contact Marilyn Thompson. She was very apologetic, but explained that the editors had decided not to go with it as a major story. Instead, they printed a brief synopsis of the tapes, and basically said, "It's nothing new."

Once again the mainstream media had chosen to deliver less than the truth to the American public. Whether it's out of a desire to support the administration or a fear of reprisal and decreased access to the White House, the result is the same . . . the public is getting shortchanged. I believe that Americans should have the right to know all the facts. And those facts should be reported by the media, so that people can make informed choices. The media is not living up to its responsibility.

★ ★ ★ ★

Bill Clinton is obsessed with power. It's like an aphrodisiac to him. And his current position gives him almost unlimited power. This love of power is nothing new. In D.C. it's referred to as "Potomac Fever," and it strikes people at all levels of government. But this power fever doesn't strike only in Washington; it's a phenomenon seen all over the country . . . at the state level and even the city level. One reason that power is so attractive to men is the perks that come with it. One of the most enjoyable of those perks is that certain women are extremely attracted to the power scent and are eager to seduce or be seduced by those men with power. In many cases, the power and the increased sexual activity seem to go hand-in-hand. It's been going on for centuries, and will probably continue for centuries to come.

If, however, those women decide to talk about their liaisons with these powerful men, look out. The typical response of the media is to attack the women, do whatever they can to invalidate the story. Men, in general, get pissed that these woman would have the gall to tell their stories. Surprisingly enough, most women react the same way. But I think that's changing. In growing numbers, women are beginning to realize that it takes two to tango. And probably in the majority of cases, the man is responsible for the seduction in the first place. Besides, what gives anyone the right to censor what a person can say about his or her own life story?

I really believe that my story is part of history. And it's not over yet. Bill is still the president, and I believe there's a lot more damaging information that will be coming to light about both him and Hillary. After all, the Whitewater investigation has yet to be resolved, as do the Vince Foster intrigue and the Paula Jones suit.

I am often asked what I think happened with Vince Foster. I really don't know whether he committed suicide or not. I do know that being caught up in the Clinton power structure can be heady business, but look out if you decide to cross them. Maybe Foster knew too much, maybe he was a threat to the power structure. Maybe he felt unable to face what he knew was coming when information about Whitewater and other issues began to surface. Whatever the truth is, I can certainly relate to his situation. In fact, during some bleak times, the thought of suicide crossed my mind. But I'm too much of a survivor to make that choice. His story also adds to my fear for my own safety. At any time in the last few years, I could have been killed, and it could have been made to look like suicide.

★ ★ ★ ★

Public reaction to my story has been interesting. Not only has the media tried to suppress information, they've also reported outrageous lies about me. Sometimes I have to laugh at the things they report. I was watching the *Joan Rivers Show* one day, sitting in my apartment in Dallas, and a well-known columnist came on and said she knew for a fact that at that moment I was in Japan, singing. I had to laugh. Dallas is about as far from Japan as you can get.

In 1992, Finis and I attended the Thalian Ball in Hollywood, and a well-respected weekly news magazine reported that although I sat there quietly, enjoying the festivities, I certainly made a point because my escort was wearing a Bill Clinton mask! I *was* there, and a few people *were* wearing masks, but no one at our table was wearing one, and certainly not Finis. The story was a complete fabrication. Although when Finis read the article, he laughed and said he wished he'd thought of wearing a Clinton mask!

Finis called me after returning from a trip to San Antonio and asked if I had been there recently. He had seen a picture of Bill Clinton in a restaurant and teasingly remarked to the owner that he really needed a picture of Gennifer Flowers to put up on the wall next to Bill. The restaurant owner didn't know Finis' connection to me, and he told him I had been in the restaurant the previous weekend and he had taken a picture of me; he just hadn't gotten it developed yet. I've never been to San Antonio, either.

After the story broke in the *Star*, people came out of the woodwork claiming a connection with Bill and me. One woman said she had flown to Mexico on a Lear jet with Bill and me. Another woman swore she and her boyfriend spent a great deal of time socializing with Bill and me and provided details about the places we went together. Interesting. During the entire twelve years Bill and I were together, we never once went out in public as a couple. We never socialized with *anyone* as a couple.

A well-educated, professional man, who lives in the same building as I do, told a friend of mine he personally saw the Secret Service pull up in the garage of the building. He claimed they cleared the area, made everyone leave, but he saw Bill Clinton get out of the car and go up to my apartment. This was after Bill was elected president!

I would be lying if I said I didn't occasionally enjoy some perks as a result of my notoriety, though. The European trips were fabulous, and I must admit I rarely have trouble getting a table in a restaurant or club, even if it's packed with people. I often get seated in the VIP section of clubs, like the House of Blues in New Orleans. Finis and I went in there one night and were seated in the same section as Kim Basinger and Alec Baldwin. It's an extremely popular place with lines out the door of people waiting to get in. We were escorted past the line and right into the restaurant as guests of the owner.

Every once in awhile, something spontaneous and totally unexpected will happen that gives me a warm feeling. My mother and I attended the Thalian Ball in Hollywood in October 1994. The ball is the main fund-raiser for the Thalian Mental Health Center at the Cedar-Sinai Medical Center. Debbie Reynolds is the president of the fund-raiser and Ruta Lee is the Board Chair. Each year the benefit honors a Mr. or Ms. Wonderful, usually someone in the entertainment business. Past honorees have included Angela Lansbury, Jimmy Stewart and Liza Minelli.

The year Mother and I attended, dozens of Hollywood stars were there, and they were all introduced, one by one. I was also introduced and, to my surprise, the applause was thunderous. I thought maybe it was my imagination, but later that week newspaper accounts of the Ball all mentioned that I received the most enthusiastic applause of the evening. I took it as a sign of growing dissatisfaction in Hollywood with liberal politics.

Two years earlier, when Finis and I attended the Ball, I had received even more press coverage. I remember we got in line with other celebrities, and at the top of the escalator that went down to the ballroom, staff members stopped us and pulled us apart from the others. We didn't know why until they asked the others to stand back and escorted us down alone. It turned out the press had been waiting for *me*. There were 60 or 70 reporters there waiting to ask me questions and snap my picture. The attitude at that time, however, was very pro-Clinton, and I got the impression that most of the celebrities in attendance resented the attention I got. It's funny how two years (and lots of shocking revelations) can change a society's feelings about its leaders.

I feel like, in some ways, my story helped bring about that change in sentiment. It was the seed that began to plant doubt in people's minds about Bill's character. At first, people were reluctant to believe me. Then, as things began to unfold and more and more stories started to come out about him and his dealings, people starting taking a closer look. I began hearing things like, "We should have known." Without my story, and it's corroborating evidence, it would have taken people much longer to unearth the truth about Bill.

When Republicans soundly defeated Democrats in elections around the country, I actually cried, because I felt that I had played a part in opening people's eyes to the truth. As I spoke on talk shows around the country over the past two years, people would ask me, "What can we do?" And I would tell them, "We can vote. We live in a democracy where we are free to choose our leaders." I told them to form groups, write letters, let others know how they felt. And that's just what happened. They sent a message to Congress saying "We want change."

★   ★   ★   ★

My life today is so different from what it was three years ago. I still get lots of offers to do various things, mostly in relation to Bill, and I'll do them if they appeal to me or sound like they might be fun. For example, on Bill's birthday I did a parody of Marilyn Monroe's "Happy Birthday Mr. President" tribute to John F. Kennedy at the request of Comedy Central. I was flown to New York and spent four or five hours being made up to look like Marilyn. My hair was styled like hers, and they found a dress that was similar to the one she wore.

I sang "Happy Birthday" and then sang a satirical little ditty composed by the Comedy Central writers. We cut a cake for him, and then I held a little press conference. Someone asked me how I thought Bill would take it, and I said I thought he'd get a chuckle out of it—privately of course. Then I was asked if I thought Hillary would laugh. Had I been thinking, I would have said I hoped she had a sense of humor, too. But instead I blurted out, that I didn't really care what she thought.

Another appearance I agreed to do was for *He Said, She Said*, a satirical magazine that devoted an issue to my affair with Bill. The publishers, First Amendment Publishing, sent me a copy and asked for my endorsement. I read the magazine and thought it was hilarious, so I agreed to attend a signing at a book store in New York. It was scheduled to last two hours, but the crowd was much bigger than they expected and so enthusiastic that I just stayed until I'd signed every copy. It took four hours and I signed over seven hundred copies of that magazine.

A friend had gone with me, and, during the signing, had a minor disagreement with a woman who was waiting in line. The woman insisted I was Ivana Trump! My friend assured her I truly was Gennifer Flowers, and all the signs in the bookstore said Gennifer Flowers, but the woman was insistent. She said "I know Ivana Trump when I see her, and that's Ivana Trump!" At least *she* didn't accuse me of being Hillary Clinton.

I thank the good Lord I've been able to maintain my sense of humor. There are times when the absurdity of everything that has happened makes me laugh out loud. And I'm not above poking fun at myself, either. I have a life-sized cardboard image of Bill that I keep in my apartment. It's quite realistic and at first glance can be mistaken for an actual person. I can't even remember why I acquired it, but one evening I decided to have some fun with it.

I was going out with some girlfriends, and I insisted they come to my apartment before we were to leave. I set my "Cardboard Bill" up in the foyer, and when I opened the door the girls came in and were face to face with Bill Clinton! I casually said, "Have you ladies met Bill Clinton?" And for the fraction of a second before they realized he wasn't real, the look of astonishment on their faces was priceless!

My little joke backfired on me, though, later that evening. I had left Bill standing in the foyer and forgot all about him by the time I came home. I opened my door, and for a brief instant thought Bill was standing there, waiting for me. I let out a scream before I remembered what it was. The shock of thinking he was there took ten years off my life. When I recovered, I gathered Bill up and stored him, face against the wall, in my garage. I didn't want any more surprises like that.

I hope someday to be able to sing professionally again. Even though I have achieved a moderate level of financial security, I miss being out there, doing what I love best. I miss the business end of it, too. That was one of the facets of my personality that Bill admired the most. I had a creative talent, but I was also capable of being in control of the practical end of my business. Bill once said to me, "You and I are so much alike. We both are driven to succeed."

That's true, we are both driven to succeed and his drive has taken him into the White House. Bill is bumping heads with the national good ol' boys now, and they are just as powerful, just as strong, and just as cunning as he is, and like him, they have big money behind them. He thought he would be able to establish a power structure in Washington like he did in Arkansas, but he's way out of his league. It's turned into a real battle for him. They win a round, he wins a round; but in the end, I think he may lose. I don't know whether or not he'll be re-elected, but I doubt it.

In a lot of ways, I think things have turned out better for me than they have for him. He may be the president of the United States, but he doesn't look like a happy or secure man. I've certainly had some demoralizing low points throughout this whole ordeal, but my perspective is a little different. I'm not dealing with the problems of a nation, only my own difficulties in getting through another day. And in retrospect, I probably wouldn't change a whole lot that's happened to me.

I have learned who is really important in my life: the friends and family members who have stood by me and provided unwavering support in spite of any doubts they might have had about me or my motives. My parents have been there every step of the way. They haven't hesitated to express their opinions, and oftentimes they disagreed with me, but their support has never been conditional.

My dear friend Margie Moore has been a rock in a stormy sea. Since the day I met her in the Cipango Club in Dallas, she has been a loyal and trustworthy friend who has never let me down. And, of course, there's Finis. He had to overcome a lot of doubts about me, and I'm the first to admit that in the beginning I was less than honest with him about my relationship with Bill. Even though we broke up for a couple of years, by the grace of God he never went too far away.

Everything that has happened in relation to my affair with Bill has combined to make me the woman I am today, good or bad. It has taken every ounce of the sweetness and the sorrow to mold me into this person and to provide me with the knowledge and experience I have gained. For all the heartache, each and every thing has contributed to making me Gennifer with a "G."

I wonder sometimes what it would be like to see Bill again and talk to him. So much has happened between us in the past three years, and yet we've never had the opportunity to share our thoughts or feelings about it. I daydream sometimes about what that might be like. All the emotions I have had—sadness, anger, frustration—I'm sure he has had too. I have hated many of the things he and his troops have done to me, and I'm sure he isn't happy with every choice I've made.

I really loved Bill, and I believed he loved me, too. I thought what we had was a real relationship between two passionate, caring people, but I learned otherwise. In the end, he turned out to be nothing more than a Cardboard Bill . . . a flat, two-dimensional piece of hardened paper, empty of all feelings.

So, like the cardboard cutout of him I have stored in my garage, I will pack away the real Cardboard Bill, and all the memories that go with him, and move onto the next stage of my life. Richer for having known him? A little. And wiser? Most definitely.